Beaded

Ornaments

for the Holidays and Beyond

from *Bead&Button* and *BeadStyle* Magazines

KALMBACH BOOKS

Kalmbach Books
21027 Crossroads Circle
Waukesha, Wisconsin 53186
www.Kalmbach.com/books

Published in 2009
13 12 11 10 09   1 2 3 4 5

Manufactured in the United States of America

ISBN: 978-0-87116-283-0

The material in this book has appeared previously
in *Bead&Button* or *BeadStyle* magazines with the
exception of the projects on pages 34, 58, 60, 66, 69,
76, 78, 84, and 92 by Diane Hertzler. *Bead&Button*
and *BeadStyle* are registered as a trademarks.

Publisher's Cataloging-in-Publication Data

Beaded ornaments : for the holidays and beyond :
from Bead&Button and BeadStyle magazines.

   p. : col. ill. ; cm.

   Contains material previously published in
Bead&Button and BeadStyle magazines.
   ISBN: 978-0-87116-283-0

1. Beadwork--Handbooks, manuals, etc. 2.
Beads--Handbooks, manuals, etc. 3. Christmas
tree ornaments--Handbooks, manuals, etc. I.
Title: Bead&Button magazine. II. Title: BeadStyle
magazine.

TT860 .B4334 2009
745.582

20

31

72

90

Introduction

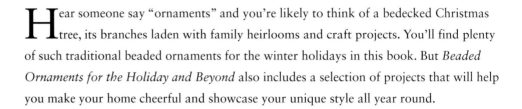

Hear someone say "ornaments" and you're likely to think of a bedecked Christmas tree, its branches laden with family heirlooms and craft projects. You'll find plenty of such traditional beaded ornaments for the winter holidays in this book. But *Beaded Ornaments for the Holiday and Beyond* also includes a selection of projects that will help you make your home cheerful and showcase your unique style all year round.

Some of the projects featured here can be used to decorate for particular holidays — the herringbone stitch pumpkin in "Pumpkin patch" (p. 69) for Halloween or Thanksgiving, the fringed heart in "Chevron heart" (p. 78) for Valentine's Day — while others are adaptable for multiple holidays, like the "Sparkling spider" (p. 43) that, depending on your color choice, can work as a Christmas or a Halloween decoration. Still other projects can work both on the Christmas tree and off — use the "Balloon ornaments" (p. 46) to decorate a Christmas tree or perhaps a baby's nursery. The ornaments included here are versatile. Try using ornaments around your home as drawer pulls and as embellishments on your door handles and drapery ties. There are plenty of great gift ideas included here as well. The netted apple in "An apple a day" (p. 34) makes an ideal gift for the teachers in your life. And the peyote stitch roll of Lifesavers (p. 92), designer Diane Hertzler tells us, is perfect to give as a thank-you present.

We've also tried to represent a variety of skill levels and beading techniques with these ornaments. Projects range from the easiest stringing projects that beginners — or beaders with minimal free time — will be able to create, to more complex stitching and netting projects that will challenge the experienced beader. These projects are collected from the pages of *BeadStyle* and *Bead&Button*, so you know they're editor tested and sure successes. Plus, *Beaded Ornaments for the Holiday and Beyond* features nine new projects that have never appeared in the magazines.

So turn the page and discover 27 projects to help you deck your home with beaded ornaments, during the holidays and beyond!

Tools and materials

Many of the projects in this book use similar beading tools and supplies to create a wide variety of different ornaments. These tools and materials are available in bead and craft stores, through catalogs, and online; sources are listed for the most hard-to-find materials in the project supply lists. Here are the more common tools and materials you'll want to be familiar with to complete most of the projects in this book.

TOOLS

Chainnose pliers have smooth, flat inner jaws, and the tips taper to a point. Use them for gripping and for opening and closing loops and jump rings.

Roundnose pliers have smooth, tapered, conical jaws used to make loops. The closer to the tip you work, the smaller the loop will be.

Crimping pliers have two grooves in their jaws that are used to fold or roll a crimp into a compact shape.

With **wire cutters**, use the front of the blades to make a pointed cut and the back of the blades to make a flat cut. Never use your jewelry wire cutters on memory wire; use heavy-duty wire cutters or bend the memory wire back and forth until it breaks.

Beading needles are coded by size. The higher the number, the finer the beading needle. Unlike sewing needles, the eye of a beading needle is almost as narrow as its shaft. In addition to the size of the

bead, the number of times you will pass through the bead also affects the needle size that you will use; if you pass through a bead multiple times, you may need to use a smaller needle.

BEADS

A huge variety of beads is available, but the beads most commonly used in the projects in this book are **seed beads.** The most common and highest quality seed beads today are manufactured in Japan or the Czech Republic. These seed beads are the most uniform and predictable in size, shape, and hole size.

Seed beads are sized by number, and range from 2° (6mm) to 24° (smaller than 1mm) — the higher the number, the smaller the bead. Bead sizes are written as a number with a symbol, such as 11/0 or 11° (pronounced "eleven aught"). The most common seed bead size is 11°, but most suppliers carry sizes ranging from 6° to 15°. Seed beads smaller than 15° are difficult to work with as their holes are tiny, and thus are hard to find.

THREAD

Threads come in many sizes and strengths. Size (diameter or thickness) is designated by a letter or number. OO, O, and A are the thinnest threads; B, D, E, F, and FF are subsequently thicker.

Plied gel-spun polyethylene (GSP), such as Power Pro or DandyLine, is made from polyethylene fibers that have been spun into two or more threads that are braided together. It is almost unbreakable, doesn't stretch, and resists fraying. The thickness can make it difficult to make multiple passes through a bead. It is ideal for stitching with larger beads, such as pressed glass and crystals.

Parallel filament GSP, such as Fireline, is a single-ply thread made from spun and bonded polyethylene fibers. It's extremely strong, doesn't stretch, and resists fraying. However, crystals will cut through parallel filament GSP, and it can leave a black residue on your hands and your beads. It's most appropriate for bead stitching.

Other threads are available, including polyester thread, such as Gutermann (best for bead crochet or bead embroidery when the thread must match the fabric); parallel filament nylon, such as Nymo or C-Lon (best used in bead weaving and bead embroidery); and plied nylon thread, such as Silamide (good for twisted fringe, bead crochet, and beadwork that needs a lot of body).

WIRE

Wire is available in a number of materials and finishes, including brass, gold, gold-filled, gold-plated, fine silver, sterling silver, anodized niobium (chemically colored wire), and copper. Brass, copper, and craft wire are packaged in 10–40-yd. (9.1–37m) spools, while gold, silver, and niobium are sold by the foot or ounce. Wire thickness is measured by gauge — the higher the gauge number, the thinner the wire — and is available in varying hardnesses (dead-soft, half-hard, and hard) and shapes (round, half-round, and square).

Flexible beading wire is composed of wires twisted together and covered with nylon. This wire is stronger than thread and does not stretch; the higher the number of inner strands (between 7 and 49), the more flexible and kink-resistant the wire. It is available in a variety of sizes. Use .014 and .015 for most gemstones, crystals, and glass beads. Use thicker varieties, .018, .019, and .024, for heavy beads or nuggets. Use thinner wire, .010 and .012, for lightweight pieces and beads with very small holes, such as pearls.

Basics
WIREWORK

Loops, plain

1 Using chainnose pliers, make a right-angle bend approximately ¼ in. (6mm) from the end of the wire.
2 Grip the tip of the wire in roundnose pliers. Press downward slightly, and rotate the wire into a loop.
3 Let go, then grip the loop at the same place on the pliers. Keep turning to close the loop.
4 The closer to the tip of the roundnose pliers that you work, the smaller the loop will be.

Loops, wrapped

1 Using chainnose pliers, make a right-angle bend approximately 1¼ in. (3.2cm) from the end of the wire.
2 Position the jaws of your roundnose pliers in the bend.
3 Curve the short end of the wire over the top jaw of the round-nose pliers.
4 Reposition the pliers so the lower jaw fits snugly in the loop. Curve the wire downward around the bottom jaw of the pliers. This is the first half of a wrapped loop.
5 To complete the wraps, grasp the top of the loop with chainnose pliers.
6 Wrap the wire around the stem two or three times. Trim the excess wire, and gently press the cut end close to the wraps with chainnose pliers.

Opening and closing plain loops and jump rings

1 Hold a loop or jump ring with two pairs of chainnose pliers or with chainnose and bentnose pliers.
2 To open the loop or jump ring, bring the tips of one pair of pliers toward you and push the tips of the other pair away.
3 Reverse the steps to close the loop or jump ring.

Crimping

1 Position the crimp bead in the hole of the crimping pliers that is closest to the handle.
2 Holding the wires apart, squeeze the tool to compress the crimp bead, making sure one wire is on each side of the dent.
3 Place the crimp bead in the front hole of the tool, and position it so the dent is facing outward. Squeeze the tool to fold the crimp in half. Tug on the wires to ensure that the crimp is secure.

STITCHES AND THREAD

Conditioning thread
Use either beeswax (not candle wax or paraffin) or Thread Heaven to condition nylon thread (Nymo). Beeswax smooths the nylon fibers and adds tackiness that will stiffen your beadwork slightly. Thread Heaven adds a static charge that causes the thread to repel itself, so don't use it with doubled thread. Stretch the thread, then pull it through the conditioner, starting with the end that comes off the spool first.

Adding thread
To add a thread, sew into the beadwork several rows prior to the point where the last bead was added. Sew through the beadwork, following the thread path of the stitch. Tie a few half-hitch knots (see **Half-hitch knot**, p. 8) between beads, and exit where the last stitch ended.

Ending thread
To end a thread, sew back into the beadwork, following the existing thread path and tying two or three half-hitch knots (see **Half-hitch knot**, p. 8) between beads as you go. Change directions as you sew so the thread crosses itself. Sew through a few beads after the last knot, and trim the thread.

Stop bead
Use a stop bead to secure beads temporarily when you begin stitching.

Choose a bead that is distinctly different from the beads in your project. String the stop bead about 6 in. (15cm) from the end of your thread, and go back through it in the same direction. If desired, go through it one more time for added security.

Brick stitch
Brick stitch naturally decreases at the start and end of each row. If you want each row to have the same number of beads, you'll need to work an increase at either the start or the end of the row.

Begin with a ladder of beads (see **Ladder stitch**), and position the thread to exit the top of the last bead. Pick up two beads, and sew under the thread bridge between the second and third beads in the previous row from back to front. Sew up through the second bead added, down through the first, and back up through the second bead.

For the row's remaining stitches, pick up one bead per stitch. Sew under the next thread bridge in the previous row from back to front, and sew back up through the new bead. The last stitch in the row will be positioned above the last two beads in the row below, creating a decrease.

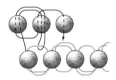

To increase at the beginning of a row, work as explained above, but start by sewing under the thread bridge between the first and second beads in the previous row.

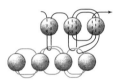

To increase at the end of the row, add a second stitch to the final thread bridge in the previous row.

Right-angle weave

To start the first row, pick up four beads, and tie them into a ring. Sew through the first three beads again.

Pick up three beads. Sew through the last bead of the previous ring again (a–b) and continue through the first two picked up in this stitch (b–c).

Continue adding three beads for each stitch until the first row is the desired length. You are sewing rings in a figure

8 pattern, alternating direction with each stitch.

To begin row 2, sew through the last three beads of the last stitch on row 1, exiting the bead at the edge of one long side.

Pick up three beads, and sew through the bead you exited in the previous step (a–b). Continue through the first new bead (b–c).

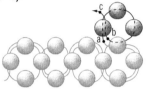

Pick up two beads, and sew through the next top bead in the previous row and the bead you exited in the previous stitch (a–b). Continue through the two new beads and the next top bead in the previous row (b–c).

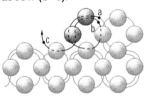

Pick up two beads, sew through the bead you exited on the previous stitch, the top bead on the previous row, and the first new bead. Keep the thread moving in a figure 8. Pick up two beads per stitch for the rest of the row. Don't sew straight lines across stitches.

Peyote: flat even-count

Pick up an even number of beads (a–b). These beads will shift to form the first two rows as you stitch the next row.

To begin row 3, pick up a bead, skip the last bead strung in the previous step, and sew back through the next bead (b–c). For each stitch, pick up a bead, skip a bead in the previous row, and sew through the next bead, exiting the first bead strung (c–d). The beads added in this row are higher than the previous rows and are referred to as "up-beads."

For each stitch in subsequent rows, pick up a bead, and sew through the next up-bead in the previous row (d–e). To count peyote stitch rows, count the total number of beads along both straight edges.

Peyote: tubular

Pick up an even number of beads to equal the desired circumference. Tie the thread and tail to form a ring, leaving some slack.

Put the ring over a form if desired. Sew through the first bead to the left of the knot. Pick up a bead, skip a bead in the previous round, and sew through the next bead. Repeat until you're back at the start.

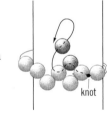

Since you started with an even number of beads, you need to work a step-up to be in position for the next round: Sew through the first bead on rounds 2 and 3. Pick up a bead, and sew through the second bead in round 3; continue.

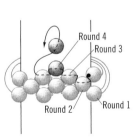

If you begin with an odd number of beads, you won't need to step up; the beads form a continuous spiral.

Basics

Zipping up or joining flat peyote

To invisibly join two sections of a flat peyote piece, match up the two pieces so the edge beads fit together. "Zip up" the pieces by zigzagging through the up-beads on both edges.

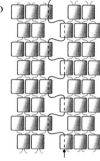

Herringbone stitch: tubular

To work tubular herringbone, you can start with either a ring or a ladder. To start with a ring, pick up the desired number of beads, and tie the tail and working thread together to form a ring.

To start with a ladder (see **Ladder stitch**), use an even number of beads, and stitch the first bead to the last bead to form a ring.

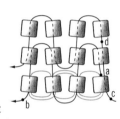

Pick up two beads, and sew through the next bead on the previous row (the ladder). Sew up through the next bead, and repeat. There will be two stitches when you've gone down through the fourth bead (**a–b**).

You need to work a step-up to be in position to start the next row. To do this, sew up through the bead next to the one your needle is exiting and the first bead of the first stitch in the row above (**c–d**).

Continue adding two beads per stitch and stepping up at the end of each round.

Ladder stitch

Traditional method

Pick up two beads, sew through the first bead again (**a–b**), and then sew through the second bead (**b–c**).

To add subsequent beads, pick up one bead, sew through the previous bead, and then sew through the new bead (**c–d**). Continue for the desired length.

This technique produces uneven tension along the ladder of beads because of the alternating pattern of a single thread bridge on one edge between two beads and a double thread bridge on the opposite edge between the same two beads. You can easily correct the uneven tension by zigzagging back through the

beads in the opposite direction. This creates a double thread path along both edges of the ladder and aligns the beads right next to each other. However, it fills the bead holes with extra thread, which can cause a problem if you are using beads with small holes.

Crossweave method

Center a bead on a length of thread with a needle attached to each end.

Working in crossweave technique, pick up a bead with one needle, and cross the other needle through it (**a–b** and **c–d**). Add all subsequent beads in the same manner.

Alternative method

Pick up all the beads you need to reach the length your pattern requires. Fold the last two beads so they are parallel, and sew through the second-to-last bead again in the same direction (**a–b**).

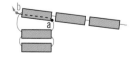

Fold the next loose bead so it sits parallel to the previous bead in the ladder, and sew through the loose bead in the same direction (**a–b**). Continue sewing back through each bead until you exit the last bead of the ladder.

Forming a ring

If you are working in tubular brick or herringbone stitch, sew your ladder into a ring to provide a base for the new technique: With your thread exiting the last bead in the ladder, sew through the first bead and then through the last bead again, or cross the needles through the first bead if you are using crossweave technique.

KNOTS

Half-hitch knot

Pass the needle under the thread between two beads. A loop will form as you pull the thread through. Cross over the thread between the beads, sew through the loop, and pull gently to draw the knot into the beadwork.

Square knot

Cross the left-hand end of the thread over the right, and bring it around and back up. Cross the end that is now on the right over the left, go through the loop, and pull both ends to tighten.

Surgeon's knot

Cross the left-hand end of the thread over the right. Tuck the same end through the loop you just made again. Pull the ends to tighten. Cross the end that is now on the right over the left, go through the loop, and tighten.

Ornament hangers

Give your ornaments an additional personalized touch by making your own ornament hangers. Put together simple, eye-catching hooks and loops four different ways. Start with a basic S-hook, add beads, and then try your hand at colorful beaded loops or hangers embellished with names or holiday messages.

materials

S-hook
- 4 in. (10cm) 20-gauge craft wire
- ⅜-in. (1cm) dowel or lid from a tube of beads
- roundnose pliers
- wire cutters

embellished S-hook
- 4g size 6º seed beads
- 5 in. (13cm) 18-gauge craft wire
- chainnose pliers

- roundnose pliers
- wire cutters

hanger with a message
- 2 6–8mm bicone crystals
- 4–6 5–6mm alphabet beads
- 4 4–5mm large-hole beads
- 4½ in. (11.4cm) 18-gauge wire, half-hard
- bench block or anvil (optional)
- chainnose pliers
- hammer (optional)

- roundnose pliers
- wire cutters

beaded-loop hanger
- 2g size 11º to 8º seed beads
- crimp bead
- crimp cover
- flexible beading wire, .014 or .015
- chainnose pliers
- crimping pliers
- wire cutters

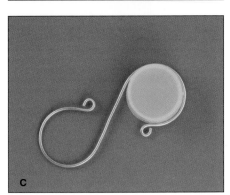

S-hook

by **Diane Hertzler**

[1] Cut a 4-in. (10cm) piece of 20-gauge wire.

[2] Grasp the end of the wire with roundnose pliers at the narrow end of the jaws and turn one loop (photo a). Repeat at the other end of the wire.

[3] Wrap the end of the wire around a dowel or the lid of a tube of beads (photo b). Repeat at the other end of the wire (photo c).

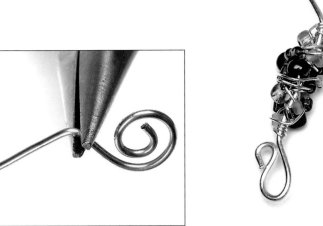

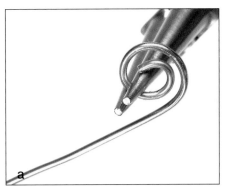

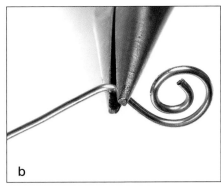

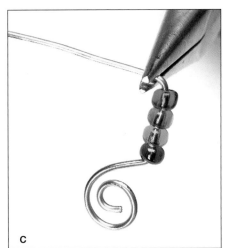

Embellished S-hook

by **Paulette Biedenbender**

[1] Cut a 5-in. (13cm) piece of 18-gauge wire. Use roundnose pliers to make a spiral loop as shown (photo a).

[2] Bend the wire at an angle using chainnose pliers (photo b).

[3] String four 6° seed beads, and bend the wire at an angle above the top bead (photo c).

[4] Bend the wire around the base of the roundnose pliers to form a large hook (photo d). Trim the wire even with the top bead.

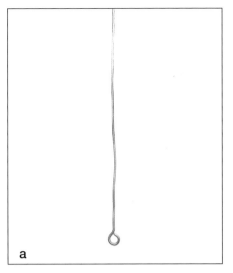

a

b

c

d

DESIGN GUIDELINES:
Instead of stringing alphabet or seed beads on the wire hanger, use 26-gauge wire to wrap seed beads around the hanger for a sculptured look (opposite page).

Hanger with a message

by **Steven James**

[1] Cut a 4½-in. (11.4cm) piece of 18-gauge wire. Make a plain loop (Basics, p. 6) on one end (photo a).

[2] String a 4–5mm bead, a bicone crystal, a 4–5mm, alphabet beads to spell the desired word, a 4–5mm, a bicone, and a 4–5mm. Bend the wire around one jaw of your roundnose pliers (photo b).

[3] Bend the wire end upward and make a loop. Trim the excess wire (photo c).

[4] If you prefer a textured look, hammer the wire gently on a bench block or anvil (photo d). Flip the hanger over and hammer the other side. Open the bottom loop (Basics) and attach the loop of an ornament. Close the loop.

a

b

c

Beaded-loop hanger

by **Steven James**

[1] Cut a 10-in. (25cm) piece of flexible beading wire. String about 5 in. (13cm) of seed beads. String each end through a crimp bead, going in opposite directions **(photo a)**.

[2] On one end, string 1½ in. (3.8cm) of seed beads and go back through the crimp bead **(photo b)**.

[3] String each end through two or three beads adjacent to the crimp bead **(photo c)**. Tighten the wire, and crimp the crimp bead (Basics). Trim the excess wire. Use chainnose pliers to close a crimp cover over the finished crimp.

[4] To attach the hanger to an ornament: Gently squeeze the ornament's wire loop to remove it. String the small beaded loop of the hanger, and replace the wire loop **(photo d)**.

d

Stringing
and Wirework

Decorate with
beaded wreaths

by **Naomi Fujimoto**

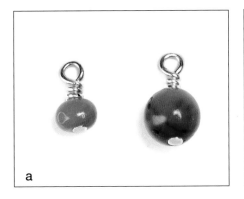

a

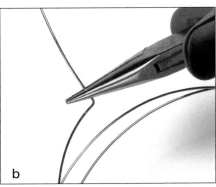

b

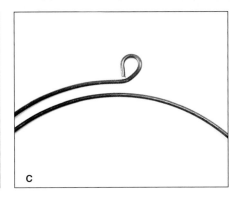

c

d

e

f

These simple wreath ornaments brighten holiday trees or gifts. If you want a wreath design that's less yuletide and more you, string whatever combination of beads you like — just make sure they have holes large enough to accommodate the memory wire.

step by step

[1] On a head pin, string a 3mm bead. Make a wrapped loop (Basics, p. 6). Repeat with a 5mm bead **(photo a)**. Make six 3mm-bead units and three 5mm-bead units.

[2] Separate one-and-a-half coils of memory wire from a stack of coils. Hold the wire with chainnose pliers, and bend it back and forth at one place until the wire breaks **(photo b)**. You also can use heavy-duty wire cutters. Do not use jewelry-weight wire cutters.

[3] Using roundnose pliers, make a small loop on one end of the memory wire **(photo c)**.

[4] String a 6º seed bead and an 18mm round bead. Repeat seven times, substituting a cluster (two 3mm units and one 5mm unit) for the 6º **(photo d)** three times. End with a 6º.

[5] Trim the wire to ½ in. (1.3cm). Make a loop next to the last bead **(photo e)**.

[6] Cut a 12-in. (30cm) piece of ribbon. String it through both loops and tie a bow. Cut a 5-in. (13cm) piece of flexible beading wire. String it through both loops **(photo f)**. String both ends through a crimp bead, and crimp the crimp bead (Basics). Trim the excess ribbon and wire.

materials
- 8 18mm round beads
- 3 5mm red round beads
- 6 3mm red round beads
- 6 size 6º seed beads
- 9 1½-in. (3.8cm) head pins
- crimp bead
- flexible beading wire, .014 or .015
- memory wire, bracelet diameter
- 12 in. (30cm) ribbon, ¾ in. (1.9cm) wide
- chainnose pliers
- crimping pliers
- heavy-duty wire cutters (optional)
- roundnose pliers
- wire cutters

DESIGN GUIDELINES:
- Make a cream-colored wreath with vintage pearls, crystals, and seed beads. Tie a bow with a pale-colored ribbon.
- Try a wreath with different shades of green (the version with the purple ribbon on p. 14 uses 8mm round beads and 9mm rondelles).

A few of our favorite things

by **Naomi Fujimoto**

a

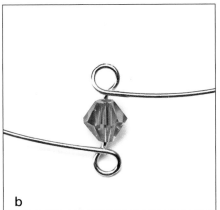

b

c

d

e

materials

all projects
- chainnose pliers
- roundnose pliers
- wire cutters

pillow ornament
- 1-in. (2.5cm) glass pillow bead (Olive Glass, oliveglass.com)
- **4 or more** 4–7mm crystals
- **2 or more** 4–5mm spacers
- 6–9 in. (15–23cm) 24-gauge craft or gold-filled wire
- 5½ in. (14cm) chain, 3mm or larger links
- 1½-in. (3.8cm) decorative head pin (optional)

icicle ornament
- glass squiggle bead, approximately 3 in. (7.6cm) long (Olive Glass)
- **4–8** 3–8mm crystals
- **1–4** 3–6mm spacers
- 12–15 in. (30–38cm) 24-gauge craft or gold-filled wire
- 5½ in. (14cm) chain, 3mm or larger links
- 2-in. (5cm) decorative head pin (optional)
- twisted-wire beading needle

egg-shaped ornament
- egg-shaped blown glass bead, approximately 20 x 24mm (Olive Glass)
- 8mm round crystal
- 6mm round crystal
- 7mm spacer
- 2½ in. (6.4cm) 20-gauge craft or gold-filled wire, or 2½-in. (6.4cm) eye pin
- 7 in. (18cm) chain, 3mm or larger links

round ornament
- 30mm round glass bead (Olive Glass)
- **7–12** 3–8mm crystals
- **1–4** 3–6mm spacers
- 9 in. (23cm) 24-gauge craft or gold-filled wire
- 5½ in. (14cm) chain, 3mm or larger links

Candy-sized pillows and icicles bright, Egg-shaped and round glass that sparkle with light, Ornaments that take just moments to string, These are a few of our favorite things!

step by step

Pillow ornament

[1] To make a glass-bead unit, cut a 4-in. (10cm) piece of 24-gauge wire. Make a wrapped loop (Basics, p. 6) at one end. String a glass bead, crystals, and spacers as desired. Make a wrapped loop above the top bead **(photo a)**.
[2] To make a crystal unit, cut a 2-in. (5cm) piece of wire. Make the first half of a wrapped loop at one end. String a crystal and make the first half of a wrapped loop at the other end **(photo b)**.
[3] To make a dangle, string crystals and spacers on a head pin or on a spiral, as desired. (To make a spiral, follow step 2 of "Round ornament.")

Make the first half of a wrapped loop above the top bead **(photo c)**.
[4] Attach the dangle's loop to the bottom loop of the glass-bead unit. Complete the wraps **(photo d)**.
[5] Attach a loop on the crystal unit to the top loop on the glass-bead unit. Cut a 5½-in. (14cm) piece of chain. Attach each end to the crystal unit's top loop. Complete the wraps **(photo e)**.

- Use craft or gold-filled wire. Avoid sterling silver wire, which will tarnish in storage.
- Select tarnish-resistant chain and spacers. Vintage chain from thrift-store jewelry works well and is inexpensive. Or try colored chain (available from Inland Products, inlandproducts.com).
- To string wire through a squiggle bead: String the wire through the eye of a twisted-wire beading needle. Make a fold in the wire about 1 in. (2.5cm) from the end. Pass the needle through the bead, pushing the wire from the other end as necessary.
- Consider the size of the area you want to decorate. The pillows' small size makes them ideal for tabletop trees, while icicles enhance window space, mantels, or bigger trees.

Icicle ornament

[1] Cut a 10-in. (25cm) piece of 24-gauge wire. Gently pass the wire through the glass bead (see "Design Guidelines," above). Make a wrapped loop (Basics) at each end (photo f).
[2] Follow steps 2 and 3 of "Pillow ornament."
[3] Attach the crystal unit, the dangle, and a chain as in steps 4 and 5 of "Pillow ornament" (photo g).

Egg-shaped ornament

[1] Cut a 2½-in. (6.4cm) piece of 20-gauge wire and make a plain loop (Basics) at one end (you may also use an eye pin). To make a glass-bead unit, string an 8mm crystal, a glass bead, a spacer, and a 6mm crystal on the eye pin. Make a plain loop above the top bead (photo h).
[2] Cut a 1-in. (2.5cm) piece of chain. Open the bottom loop of the glass-bead unit and attach the chain. Close the loop (photo i).

[3] Cut a 5½-in. (14cm) piece of chain. Open the top loop of the glass-bead unit, and attach each end of the chain. Close the loop (photo j).

Round ornament

[1] Cut a 4-in. (10cm) piece of 24-gauge wire. Make a wrapped loop (Basics) at one end. String a glass bead, crystals, and spacers as desired. Make a wrapped loop above the top bead (photo k).
[2] To make a spiral, cut a 3-in. (7.6cm) piece of wire, and make a loop at one end. Position chainnose pliers across the loop to hold it in place. Using your fingers, coil the wire into a spiral (photo l), then bend the wire upward. String beads as desired. Make the first half of a wrapped loop above the top bead.
[3] Make a crystal unit as in step 2 of "Pillow ornament." Attach the spiral, the crystal unit, and a chain as in steps 4 and 5 (photo m).

f

g

h

i

j

k

l

m

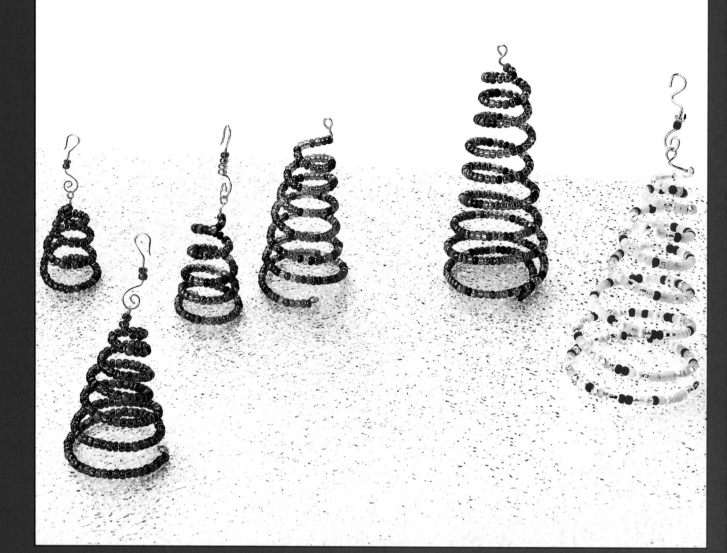

Holiday hoopla

by **Paulette Biedenbender**

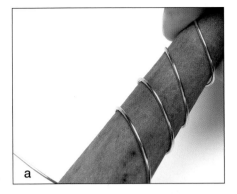

a

b

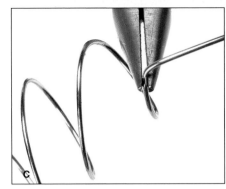

c

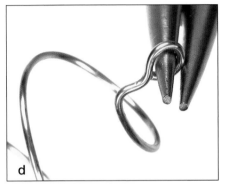

d

e

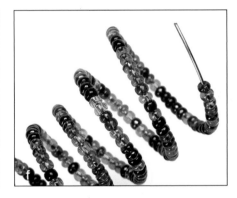

f

g

h

materials

- 2–3g size 6º seed beads
- 12 in. (30cm) 18-gauge craft wire
- 9-in. (23cm) wooden pestle
- chainnose pliers
- roundnose pliers
- wire cutters

As the holidays approach, the days grow shorter and my list of things to do grows longer. I can manage the shopping, cooking, and a couple of parties, but where do you find the time for decorating? Here's an ornament that not only works up quickly, but adds a little whimsy to your home.

step by step

[1] Hold the end of an 18-gauge wire at the narrow end of a wooden pestle, and, without cutting the wire from the spool, wind it around the pestle seven or eight times (photo a).
[2] Release the wire from the narrow end (photo b). Remove the pestle, and cut the wire from the spool after the last coil.
[3] Make a right-angle bend in the wire 1 in. (2.5cm) from the top (photo c), and make a plain loop (Basics, p. 6, and photo d).

[4] String the wire coils with 6º seed beads (photo e).
[5] Stop approximately ¾ in. (1.9cm) from the end of the wire (photo f).
[6] Using roundnose pliers, make a loop toward the inside of the coils (photo g) until it touches the last bead strung (photo h). Use your fingers to adjust the ornament's shape, if necessary.
[7] Thread a ribbon or wire hook (see "Ornament hangers," p. 9) through the top loop to hang your tree.

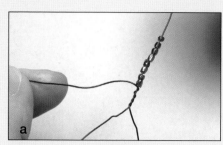

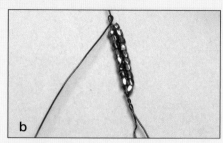

Poinsettia ornament

by **Trude Janofsky**

Making beaded flowers has been my hobby for many years. I initially designed this poinsettia to be a potted plant, then adapted it so it could be used as an ornament. It can also be made into a brooch.

stepbystep

Petals and leaves

[1] Transfer four strands of color A three-cut seed beads onto 26-gauge wire that's on a spool. Don't cut the wire off the spool.

[2] Make a bend in the wire 7 in. (18cm) from the end. Twist the wire around itself several times 4 in. (10cm) from the end, leaving a 3–4-in. (7.6–10cm) tail. The tail will be referred to as the stem. String eight or nine As from the hank on the stem **(photo a)**. This is the base row. Bend the tip of the stem to prevent the beads from falling off.

[3] Slide 10 to 11 As to the spot where the working wire (that's attached to the spool) meets the stem. Bring the working wire up, and wrap it once around the stem **(photo b)**. These petals are pointed at the top and bottom, so wrap the wire at a sharp angle to form the points.

[4] Slide 12 to 13 As along the working wire, and guide them along the other side of the base row. Wrap the working wire around the twisted wire at a sharp angle, as before **(photo c)**. Repeat this step, adding one or two As to each row until you have five rows across the petal. Trim the working wire.

[5] To finish the petal, cut one side of the wire loop below the twist **(photo d)**. Straighten the wire to form a stem. Trim the bent wire at the other end to ⅜ in. (1cm) above the petal, and bend it against the wrong side of the beadwork **(photo e)**.

materials

- **7** 3mm gold beads
- hank size 9º or 10º three-cut seed beads, in each of **2** colors:
  A, luster red or light yellow
  B, luster green
- spool 26-gauge craft wire (or **2** spools, in each of **2** colors: A, B)
- spool 28-gauge gold craft wire
- 1 yd. (.9m) 34-gauge craft wire (optional)
- 18 in. (46cm) ¼–⅜ in.-wide (6–10mm) ribbon
- 8 in. (20cm) decorative cord (optional)
- glue
- green floral tape
- chainnose pliers
- wire cutters

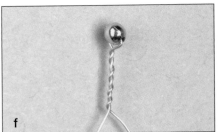

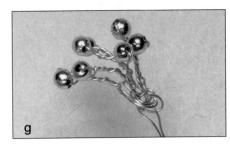

[6] Repeat steps 2–5 to make a total of five small petals.

[7] Make a large petal as in steps 2–5, but start with 15 or 16 As. Make a total of five large petals.

[8] Transfer two strands of color B three-cut seed beads onto 26-gauge wire that's on a spool. Make a leaf, following the instructions for the large petals, but work seven rows across. Make a total of five leaves.

Center

[1] String seven 3mm beads on 28-gauge wire that's on a spool. Slide one 3mm to 3 in. (7.6cm) from the end, hold the 3mm, and twist the wire around itself a few times against the bead. Keep the twists close together. Don't trim the wire off the spool (photo f).

[2] Slide another 3mm about 1 in. (2.5cm) from the twist. Hold the bead and twist the wire. Repeat with the remaining five 3mms.

[3] Gather the base of each twist. Twist the bases together (photo g). Cut the wire from the spool, leaving a 3-in. (7.6cm) tail after the last twist.

Assembly

[1] Gather the five small petals and the 3mms. Twist their stems together for about ⅝ in. (1.6cm), working close to the beads.

[2] Arrange the petals so they radiate around the 3mms in the center, keeping their right sides facing up (photo h).

[3] Place the large petals behind and between the small petals one at a time, wrapping each wire around the stem. If you have 34-gauge wire, wrap it around the assembled stems several times to keep them in place (photo i).

[4] Add the leaves behind and between the large petals (photo j), wrapping the wires around the stem as before.

[5] Trim the stem to 2¼ in. (5.7cm), cutting at a slight angle across the

bottom. Twist the wires tightly together using pliers (photo k).

[6] Cut the end of a piece of floral tape at an angle, and place it against the stem at the base of the beads. Stretch the tape slightly as you wrap so the tape will adhere to itself (photo l).

[7] Shape each petal and each leaf individually by lifting slightly at the center and pushing down on the tip to curve it.

[8] Cover the floral tape with ribbon, and curl the stem into a coil (photo m). Dab the ribbon's end with glue to keep it from unraveling. Add a bow, if desired.

[9] Thread a ribbon or wire hook (see "Ornament hangers," p. 9) through one of the leaves or petals to hang your flower.

Andromeda
ornament

by **Judy Heller**

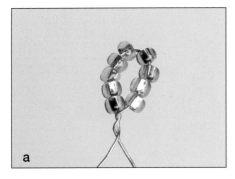

a

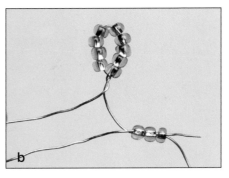

b

c

d

e

f

Making beaded flowers has been a tradition in my family for several generations; I learned how to make them from my mother more than 30 years ago, and I still love it. This andromeda ornament uses two French beaded-flower techniques: continuous loops for the flower clusters and round bottom, pointed top for the leaves.

stepbystep

Flower clusters

[1] String three strands of color A three-cut beads onto a spool of color A wire. Don't cut the wire from the spool.

[2] To start the flower, slide nine beads 4 in. (10cm) from the end of the wire, make a loop, and twist twice **(photo a)**.

[3] Slide three beads next to the twist and thread the 4-in. (10cm) wire tail through them **(photo b)**.

[4] Make another nine-bead loop as close as you can to the three beads added in step 3. Instead of twisting the wire as before, wrap the working wire around the back of the loop and bring it to the front between the three beads and the loop **(photo c)**.

[5] Slide another three beads next to the new loop and thread the tail through them, as in step 3.

[6] Repeat steps 4 and 5. Once you've gone through the beads after the third loop, trim the tail close to the beads.

[7] For each remaining loop, slide 12 beads to the previous loop, form a new loop, and wrap the working wire twice between the third and fourth bead strung. Continue until you've completed the 12 loops required for Unit 1. Leave about 5 in. (13cm) of wire, and cut the unit from the spool. Make a total of seven flower units as follows:

Unit 1: 12 loops, 3 beads between loops.
Unit 2: 10 loops, 3 beads between loops.
Unit 3: 8 loops, 3 beads between loops.
Unit 4: 6 loops, 3 beads between loops.
Unit 5: 9 loops, 1 bead between loops.
Unit 6: 7 loops, 1 bead between loops.
Unit 7: 4 loops, 1 bead between loops.

Leaves

[1] String four strands of color B three-cut beads onto a spool of color B wire. Don't cut the wire from the spool.

[2] With the end 7 in. (18cm) of wire, make a 2-in. (5cm) loop, and twist several times to close the loop, leaving a 3-in. (7.6cm) tail.

materials

- hank size 9º three-cut seed beads, in each of **2** colors:
  A, gold
  B, green
- 26-gauge artistic wire, in each of **2** colors:
  A, gold
  B, green
- 12–18 in. (30–46cm) wire-edge ribbon, ⅞ in. (2.2cm) wide
- 2 ft. (61cm) gold cord (optional)
- double-sided tape
- floral tape
- glass ornament
- wire cutters

[3] Slide eight beads against the twisted loop, and secure them with another twisted loop **(photo d)**. Trim the 3-in. (7.6cm) tail flush against the beads. The eight beads between loops are called the "bead base" and comprise row 1.

[4] Hold the working wire at a right angle to the bead base. This is the stem end (bottom) of the leaf. Slide enough beads along the wire to wrap one side of the bead base **(photo e)**. Bring the beads alongside the bead base and push them into position against the bottom loop. The wire must be angled upward at about 45 degrees to create a pointed leaf (photo f). This is row 2. (Rows are counted across the leaf.) Keep the rows close together.

[5] Slide beads into position for row 3. Bring the beads to the bottom loop along the other side of the bead base. Wrap the wire around the bottom of the leaf at a right angle (photo g).

[6] Repeat steps 4 and 5 until you've made five rows. Clip the twist at the pointed end (the tip of the leaf) about ¼ in. (6mm) from the beads, and fold it against the back. Leave about 5 in. (13cm) of working wire after the last row, and cut the leaf from the spool. Make a total of 10 leaves as follows:
Leaf 1: 8-bead base, 5 rows. Make 5.
Leaf 2: 8-bead base, 7 rows. Make 5.

Flower assembly

[1] Twist together the following four flower clusters: Unit 1 (12 loops), Unit 3 (eight loops), Unit 5 (nine loops), and Unit 6 (seven loops) (photo h). Twist the remaining clusters into a second group.

[2] Twist both groups together, and wrap the wire stem with floral tape, stretching the tape as you wrap. Wrap the tape at an angle as you work down the wires (photo i).

[3] Wrap the stem of each leaf with floral tape. Wrap each leaf to the flower stem, placing the smaller leaves on top. Space them evenly all around (photo j).

Ornament assembly

[1] Place the andromeda's stem inside a glass ornament, trimming the wires to fit. If the opening is larger than the stem, wrap the stem with double-sided tape until the flower sits upright. Be very gentle or the ornament will break.

[2] Tie a ribbon around the neck of the ornament and make a bow in back. Use double-sided tape to keep the ribbon in place. If you're planning to hang the ornament, tie cord or monofilament under the ribbon.

[3] Shape the flower clusters by arranging the short clusters on top of the longer ones. Curve the leaves so they turn down in front and up in back until you're satisfied with the look.

g

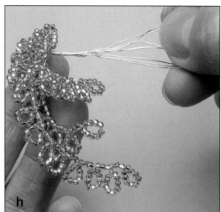
h

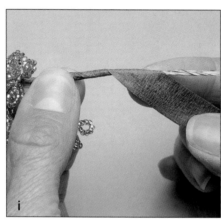
i

j

DESIGN GUIDELINES:

- Finding 90 three-cut beads can be difficult, so you may want to work with silver-lined or other reflective seed beads. If you use beads that are size 10º or smaller, use 28-gauge wire for the flower clusters. Leave a 6-in. (15cm) wire tail, and slide it through each set of beads between the loops.

- To avoid having the tail wire kink as you work, keep the beads 2–3 in. (5–7.6cm) away from the loop when you slide the tail wire through them. Then push the beads into place next to the loop. Running the second wire through the beads gives your flowers extra body and helps them retain their shape.

- Andromeda clusters can easily be modified to fit ornaments of other sizes and shapes. For example, to make a larger ornament, simply add loops to each flower cluster or increase the number of clusters.

- Change a leaf's length by increasing or decreasing the number of beads in the bead base, and change the width by adjusting the number of rows.

Ornament
Covers
and Netting

Christmas past

by **Anna Elizabeth Draeger**

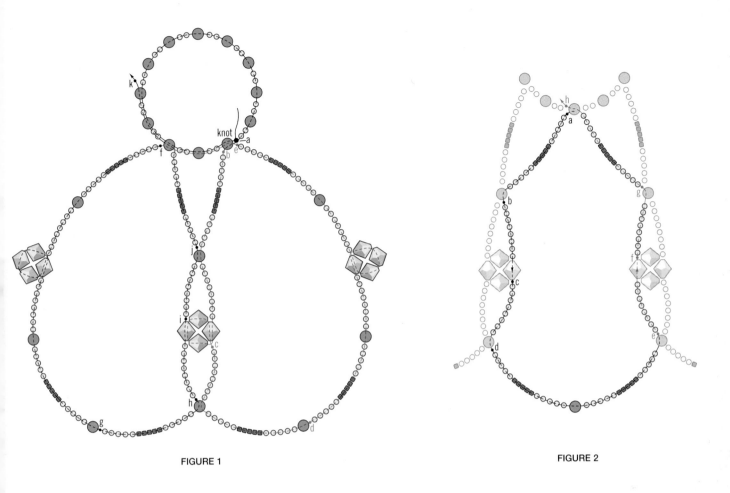

FIGURE 1

FIGURE 2

Use seed beads and crystals to bead a simple swag ornament cover for elegant holiday decorating.

stepbystep

Loops

[1] On a 4-yd. (3.7m) length of thread, center a repeating pattern of a 6º seed bead and two 11º seed beads 12 times for a total of 36 beads.

[2] Tie the beads into a ring with a surgeon's knot (Basics, p. 6). Sew back through the last 6º (**figure 1, a–b**).

[3] Pick up five 11ºs, five three-cut seed beads, five 11ºs, a 6º, eight 11ºs, and four 4mm crystals. Sew through the first 4mm again (**b–c**).

[4] Pick up eight 11ºs, a 6º, five 11ºs, five three-cuts, five 11ºs, and a 6º (**c–d**).

[5] String the second half of the loop in the mirror image of the first (**d–e**), then sew through the first 6º in the ring and through the next six beads (**e–f**).

[6] Begin the next loop as in steps 3 and 4 (**f–g**).

[7] Pick up five 11ºs, five three-cuts, and five 11ºs. Sew through the side 6º in the previous loop (**g–h**).

[8] Pick up eight 11ºs. Sew through the side 4mm in the previous loop (**h–i**).

[9] Pick up eight 11ºs. Sew through the next 6º in the previous loop (**i–j**).

[10] Pick up five 11ºs, five three-cuts, and five 11ºs. Sew through the 6º your thread exited to begin this loop and the next six beads in the ring (**j–k**).

[11] Repeat steps 6–10 to make a total of five loops.

[12] To connect the first and fifth loops, pick up five 11ºs, five three-cuts, and five 11ºs, and sew through the next 6º in the first loop (**figure 2, a–b**).

[13] Pick up eight 11ºs, and sew through the next 4mm in the first loop (**b–c**).

[14] Pick up eight 11ºs, and sew through the next 6º in the first loop (**c–d**).

[15] Pick up five 11ºs, five three-cuts, five 11ºs, a 6º, five 11ºs, five three-cuts, and five 11ºs. Sew through the adjacent 6º in the fifth loop (**d–e**).

materials

- round ball ornament, 2-in. (5cm) diameter
- bicone crystals:
  18 6mm
  66 4mm
- **36** size 6º Japanese seed beads
- hank of size 12º three-cut beads
- 15g size 11º Japanese seed beads
- nylon beading thread, conditioned with beeswax or Thread Heaven, color to match seed beads
- beading needles, #12

FIGURE 4

FIGURE 5

FIGURE 3

[16] Pick up eight 11ºs, and sew through the next 4mm in the fifth loop (e–f).
[17] Pick up eight 11ºs, and sew through the next 6º in the fifth loop (f–g).
[18] Pick up five 11ºs, five three-cuts, and five 11ºs. Sew through the 6º in the ring (g–h). Retrace the thread path through the ring. Sew through the beads, and exit a 6º at the bottom of a loop.

Closing the bottom

[1] Insert an ornament into the beadwork. Pick up two 11ºs, a 6º, and two 11ºs. Sew through the bottom 6º in the next loop.
[2] Repeat, sewing the loops together to form a ring. If necessary, adjust the number of 11ºs to make the bottom ring snug against the ornament.
[3] Retrace the thread path through the bottom ring. End the thread (Basics).

Embellishment
Top-ring fringe

[1] Thread a needle on the 2-yd. (1.8m) tail, and exit a 6º in the original ring between two loops.

[2] Pick up 15 three-cuts, an 11º, a 6mm crystal, and three 11ºs. Sew back through the 6mm and the 11º above it (figure 3, a–b).
[3] Pick up 15 three-cuts, skip five beads in the ring, and sew through the next 6º (b–c).
[4] Repeat steps 2 and 3 around the ring.

Side loops

[1] Sew through the beads to exit the first 6º above the 4mms on a loop (figure 3, point d).
[2] Pick up 15 11ºs, a 4mm, and 15 11ºs. Sew through the next 6º on the other side of the loop (d–e).
[3] Pick up three three-cuts, and go back through the 6º (e–f).
[4] Repeat steps 2 and 3 around the ornament, exiting at **point g**.
[5] Sew down through the next eight 11ºs and the top 4mm (g–h).
[6] Pick up 15 three-cuts, an 11º, a 4mm, an 11º, and 15 three-cuts. Sew through the top 4mm on the other side of loop (h–i).
[7] Repeat around the ornament, then sew down through the 4mm and 11ºs to

exit the next 6º (point j).
[8] Repeat steps 2 and 3 (j–k) around the ornament. End the thread.

Bottom-ring fringe

[1] Secure a new thread in the beadwork, and exit a 6º on the bottom ring (figure 4, point a).
[2] Pick up 10 three-cuts, 10 11ºs, a 4mm, a 6mm, a 4mm, and three 11ºs. Sew back through the crystals, the 11ºs, and eight three-cuts (a–b).
[3] Pick up two three-cuts, and sew through the next 6º in the ring (b–c).
[4] Pick up five three-cuts, 10 11ºs, a 4mm, a 6mm, a 4mm, and three 11ºs. Sew back through the crystals, the 11ºs, and three three-cuts (c–d).
[5] Repeat step 3 (d–e).
[6] Repeat steps 2–5 around the ring.

Outer loops

[1] Exiting a 6º on the bottom ring, pick up 25 three-cuts, skip two 6ºs, and sew through the next 6º (figure 5, a–b).
[2] Repeat step 1 three times and end the thread.

Sparkling ruffles

by **Karen E. DeSousa**

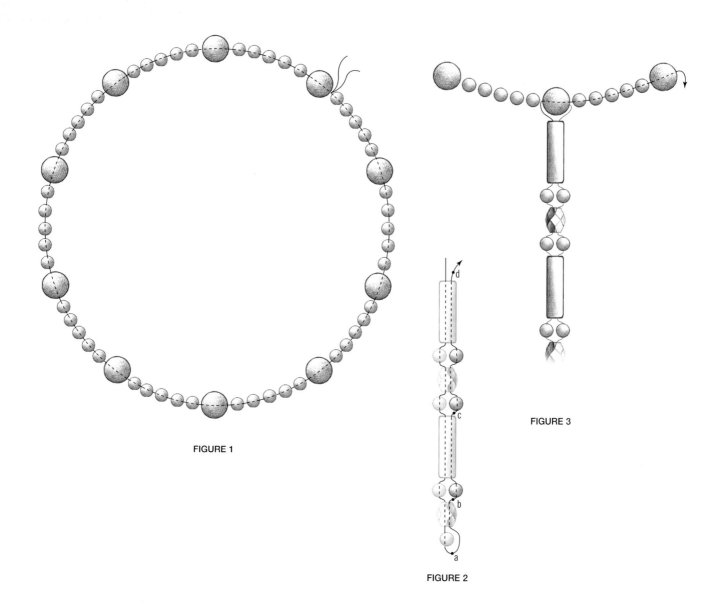

FIGURE 1

FIGURE 2

FIGURE 3

I'm a busy person with a busy life, so when I bead, I want maximum results with minimum effort. One day, I admired a gorgeous, gem-laden necklace in a jewelry store window. I thought the design could work as an ornament, so I quickly sketched my idea. Later, I tried to adjust the design to an ornament's curved shape, but, of course, it simply didn't work. What I got instead was this whimsical, ruffled effect, and I loved it.

step by step

Base

[1] On 1½ yd. (1.4m) of thread, pick up a repeating pattern of one 11º seed bead and five 14º seed beads 10 times, leaving a 6-in. (15cm) tail.

[2] Tie the beads into a ring **(figure 1)** with a square knot (Basics, p. 6), and sew through the first seven beads again.

[3] Pick up a repeating pattern of a bugle bead, a 14º, a 4mm fire-polished bead, and a 14º seven times. Turn, skip the last 14º, and sew back through the previous 4mm **(figure 2, a–b)**.

[4] Pick up a 14º and sew through the next bugle **(b–c)**. Tighten the thread, and position the beads so the newly added 14ºs sit next to their neighboring 14ºs. Continue back **(c–d)** toward the ring, adding one 14º per stitch. Adjust the tension so the beads hang straight.

[5] When you reach the ring, sew through the 11º at the top of the rib you just made, and continue through the next six beads in the ring **(figure 3)**.

[6] Repeat steps 3–5 nine times, for a total of 10 ribs.

Ruffles

[1] To start the first lace ruffle, pick up five 14ºs, skip two 14ºs in the ring, and sew through the following 14º **(figure 4, a–b)**. Pick up five 14ºs, and sew through the next 11º in the ring

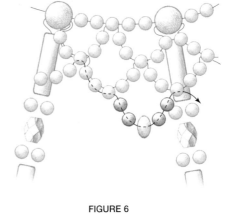

FIGURE 4

FIGURE 6

FIGURE 5

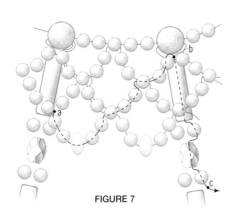

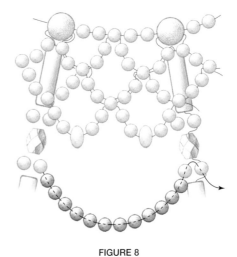

FIGURE 7

FIGURE 8

(b–c). Repeat around the ring. Sew through the first three beads added on this round **(figure 5, point a)**.

[2] Pick up five 14ºs, and sew through the third 14º in the next stitch in the previous round **(a–b)**. Repeat **(b–c)** around the ring. Step up through the first three beads added in this round.

[3] Pick up five 14ºs (or two 14ºs, a 3mm drop bead, and two 14ºs), and sew through the third 14º in the next stitch in the previous round **(figure 6)**. Repeat around the ring.

[4] To start the next ruffle, sew back through the ruffle you just made **(figure 7, a–b)**. Sew through the next bugle, 14º, 4mm, and 14º **(b–c)**.

[5] Pick up 12 14ºs. To connect the net to the next rib, sew up through the next 14º and down through the following 14º

(figure 8). Repeat around.

[6] To complete the ruffle, make four rounds of netting by repeating step 1 once, step 2 twice, and step 3 once. Sew through the beadwork as in step 4 to get into position to begin the next ruffle.

[7] Continue making ruffles with a base round and four rounds of netting as in the previous ruffle, but adjust the base rounds as follows:

Third ruffle: Pick up 18 14ºs between ribs.
Fourth ruffle: Pick up 21 14ºs between ribs.
Fifth ruffle: Pick up 21 14ºs between ribs.
Sixth ruffle: Pick up 18 14ºs between ribs.
End and add thread (Basics) as needed.

[8] Place the beadwork over an ornament. Make one more ruffle, beginning with 12 14ºs between ribs. When you finish this ruffle, sew through to the last bugle on the nearest rib. Sew

through the bugle, either 14º, and the 4mm, and exit through the bottom 14º.

[9] Pick up three to five 14ºs, and sew through the 14º at the bottom of the next rib. Repeat around the ornament, and end the thread and the tail.

materials

- round ball ornament, 2⅝-in. (6.7cm) diameter
- 10g 6mm bugle beads
- **70** 4mm fire-polished beads, in **1** or more colors
- 20g 3mm drop beads
- 10g size 11º seed beads
- 36g size 14º (or 15º) seed beads
- nylon beading thread
- beading needles, #12

An apple a day

by **Diane Hertzler**

Being married to a schoolteacher, I have had many opportunities to give a beaded apple as a gift! This apple comes together with netting used to cover the apple and peyote stitch used to weave the stem and leaf.

step by step

Prepare the apple

Prepainted wooden apples are available, but if you prefer to paint your own, they are also available unfinished.

[1] Paint a wooden apple with one coat of primer or gesso. Let it dry and lightly sand it if needed.

[2] Follow with two coats of acrylic paint, allowing time to dry between coats, and finish with a coat of varnish.

[3] Drill a 9/64 in. (3.5mm) hole through the center of the apple. Cut a drinking straw in half, and slit it lengthwise. Slide the apple onto the straw.

Beaded end rings

[1] On a comfortable length of thread, pick up 10 color A 11º seed beads, leaving a 6-in. (15cm) tail. Sew through the beads again **(figure 1)** to form a ring. Tie the working thread and tail with a square knot (Basics, p. 6). Sew through several beads, and trim. Thread a needle on the tail, sew through several beads, and trim.

[2] Slide the ring of beads over the straw to rest against the bottom end of the apple.

[3] Repeat step 1 to make another ring, but do not trim the working thread. Instead, sew through the next bead in the ring. Slide the ring over the straw to rest against the top of the apple.

Netting

[1] Bead the net over the apple as follows:
Row 1: Pick up six As and one color B 11º seed bead. Pick up a repeating pattern of five As and one B five times. Pick up two As. Sew through one A in the bottom ring **(figure 2, a–b)**.
Row 2: Sew back through the last two As and one B just picked up **(b–c)**. Pick up five As, one B, and five As. Skip the next 11 beads in the previous row, and sew through the next B **(c–d)**. Repeat **(d–e)**. Pick up five As, one B, and six As, and sew through the next A in the top ring **(e–f)**.

Row 3: Sew back through the last six As and one B just added **(f–g)**. Pick up five As, one B, and five As, skip 11 beads in the previous row, and sew through the next B **(g–h)**. Repeat **(h–i)**. Pick up five As, one B, and two As, and sew through the next A in the bottom ring **(i–j)**.
Rows 4–19: Repeat rows 2 and 3 eight times **(j–k)**.
Row 20: To work row 20, which connects row 19 to row 1, sew back through the two As and one B just added **(k–l)**. Pick up five As and sew through the next B in row 1 **(l–m)**. Pick up five As and sew through the next B in row 19 **(m–n)**. Repeat **(n–o)**. Pick up five As, and sew through the top B and six As in row 1 **(o–p)**.
[2] Sew through three beads in the top ring **(p–q)**. Sew into the netted beadwork, and end the thread and tail (Basics).

FIGURE 1

materials

- wooden apple, 1¼ x 1⅝ in. (3.2 x 4.1cm)
- 7g size 11º seed beads, color A, red
- 1g size 11º seed beads, color B, gold
- 1g size 11º seed beads, color C, green
- ½g size 11º cylinder beads, green
- 8 in. (20cm) 20-gauge craft wire
- nylon beading thread, size B, in gold, red, and green
- beading needles, #10
- acrylic paint (optional)
- artist's acrylic paintbrush, approximate size 4 (optional)
- drinking straw
- primer or gesso (optional)
- small piece of fine-grain sandpaper (optional)
- water-based, high-gloss varnish (optional)
- drill
- needlenose pliers
- roundnose pliers
- wire cutters

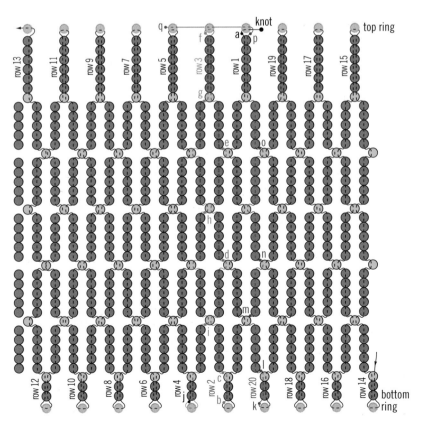

FIGURE 2

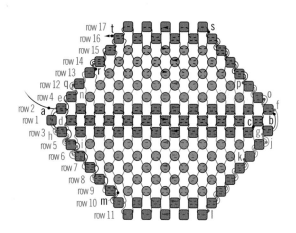

FIGURE 3

FIGURE 4

FIGURE 5

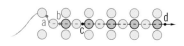

FIGURE 6

FIGURE 7

Leaf

[1] On a comfortable length of thread, pick up 23 color C cylinder beads (figure 3, a–b), leaving a 6-in. (15cm) tail. These beads make up rows 1 and 2.
[2] Work peyote stitch (Basics) as follows:
Row 3: Pick up one cylinder, skip the last cylinder picked up in the previous step, and sew through the next (b–c). Continue in peyote stitch across the row (c–d). To turn, pick up two cylinders and sew through the first cylinder picked up in step 1 (d–e).
Row 4: Row 4 will be sewn to row 2 rather than row 3: Work one stitch with a cylinder, nine stitches with C 11º seed beads, and one stitch with a cylinder (e–f). To turn, sew through the end bead in row 3 (f–g).
Row 5: Row 5 will be sewn to row 3. Work one stitch with a cylinder, nine stitches with C 11ºs, and one stitch with a cylinder (g–h). Sew under the thread between the bead just exited and the bead that sits diagonally above it. Sew back through the bead just exited and the last bead strung (h–i).
Row 6: Work one stitch with a cylinder, eight stitches with C 11ºs, and one stitch with a cylinder (i–j). Sew under the thread bridge between the bead just exited and the bead that sits diagonally above it. Sew back through the bead just exited and the last bead strung (j–k).
Rows 7–10: Work as in rows 5 and 6, decreasing as shown. In row 10, use only cylinders (k–l).

Row 11: Work five stitches with cylinders (l–m). Sew through the edge beads to exit the other side of the leaf (m–n).
Row 12: Work across the row as shown (n–o). Sew under the thread bridge between the bead just exited and the bead that sits diagonally below it. Sew back through the bead just exited and the last bead added (o–p).
Row 13: Work across the row as shown (p–q). Sew under the thread bridge between the bead just exited and the bead that sits diagonally below it. Sew back through the bead just exited and the last bead added (q–r).
Rows 14–16: Work as in rows 12 and 13, using cylinders only in row 16 (r–s).
Row 17: Work across the row with cylinders (s–t).
[3] End the thread and tail.

Stem

[1] On a comfortable length of thread, pick up 11 Bs, leaving an 18-in. (46cm) tail (figure 4, a–b).
[2] Pick up one B, skip a B, and sew through the next (figure 5, a–b). Work in peyote stitch to the end of the row (b–c), then sew through the first B picked up in the previous step (c–d).
[3] Sew through the first bead in the middle row. Sew through the first bead in row 2 (figure 6, a–b). Pick up one B and sew through the next B in the row (b–c). Continue, adding four more Bs (c–d).

[4] End the thread, but do not end the tail.

Assembly

[1] Thread a needle on the tail of the stem.
[2] Sew through two beads on the top ring of the apple (figure 7, a–b). Sew through two beads at the bottom of the stem (b–c).
[3] Retrace the thread path to reinforce the connection (c–d).
[4] Sew through seven beads on the top ring (d–e).
[5] Attach the leaf the same way you attached the stem (e–f). Retrace the thread path (f–g), and end the thread.

Hanging loop

[1] Cut an 8-in. (20cm) piece of wire. Make a wrapped loop (Basics) at one end.
[2] String the unfinished end of the wire through the top of the apple. With roundnose pliers, coil the end of the wire until it fits snugly against the bottom of the apple.
[3] Thread a ribbon or wire hanger (see "Ornament hangers," p. 9) through the wrapped loop to hang the apple.

Frosted ornaments

by **Diane Jolie**

a

b

c

Holiday decorating can always use a little extra glitz. When choosing beads for this ornament, think of it as jewelry for your home, and go all out with a sumptuous assortment of pearls and crystals. Your extravagance in this easy string-and-stitch design will reward you for years to come.

step by step

Beaded base

[1] Place your ornament on a cup or mug for stability. Measure the circumference of the ornament **(photo a)**. Cut a piece of Fireline to three times that length.

[2] String a mix of 3–6mm pearls, gems, or faceted glass beads to the circumference length. Sew through the beads again, tighten them into a ring, and check the fit. Tie a surgeon's knot (Basics, p. 6). Sew through the next few beads, then trim the working thread and the tail. Place the beaded ring on the ornament **(photo b)**.

[3] Measure the circumference of the ornament's cap. String beads to this length on 3 yd. (2.7m) of Fireline. Sew through the beads again. Form a beaded loop as before, but trim only the short tail **(photo c)**.

[4] On the working end, string beads to about seven times the ornament's circumference. Secure the end with tape. Coil the strung beads around the ornament. Remove the tape, then add or remove beads until the strand fits snugly above the beaded ring made in step 2. Tape the end again, then uncoil the strand **(photo d)**.

[5] Add a new 3-yd. (2.7m) length of Fireline (Basics) in the top ring of beads, and trim the tail. With this thread, sew through every other bead in the ring and the strand, connecting the two **(figure 1)**.

[6] Continue attaching the beaded strand to the previous round by sewing through groups of three or four beads **(figure 2)**. Attach the end of the strand to the ring made in step 2 by sewing through every other bead. End the thread **(photo e)**.

Scalloped fringe

[1] Add a new 2-yd. (1.8m) length of conditioned nylon beading thread (Basics) in the lowest ring of beads. Sew through any bead, then pick up a 4mm pearl, three 3mm pearls, a 6mm faceted bead, three 3mms, and a 4mm **(figure 3, a–b)**. Sew around the thread bridge between two beads ½ in. (1.3cm) from your starting point **(b–c)**.

[2] Sew through the last 4mm **(c–d)**, then pick up three 3mms, a 6mm, three 3mms, and a 4mm **(d–e)**.

[3] Continue adding scalloped fringe until you reach the first 4mm **(figure 4, a–b)**. Sew through the 4mm, ½ in. (1.3cm) of beads in the lowest ring, and

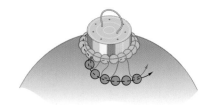

FIGURE 1

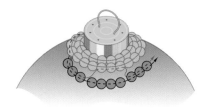

FIGURE 2

the next 4mm and 3mm in the scalloped fringe **(b–c)**.

[4] Pick up a 4mm, a 3mm, a rice pearl, a drop pearl, and a rice pearl **(c–d)**. Sew back through the 3mm and 4mm **(d–e)**, and through the 3mm and 4mm in the scalloped fringe **(e–f)**. Sew through ½ in. (1.3cm) in the ring and the next 4mm and 3mm **(f–g)**.

[5] Continue adding dangles to the fringe as in step 4.

d

e

materials

- round ball ornament, 3⅓-in. (8.5cm) diameter
- **22** 6mm faceted beads
- **5** 16-in. (41cm) strands 3–6mm pearls, gems, or faceted glass beads
- pearls, 16-in. (41cm) strand each:
  6mm drop
  4mm round
  3mm round
  3mm rice
- Fireline 10 lb. test
- nylon beading thread, white, conditioned with Thread Heaven
- beading needles, #12
- cup or mug
- tape

DESIGN GUIDELINE:

Optionally, add three 3mm pearls instead of one to every other dangle, if you have an even number of scallops.

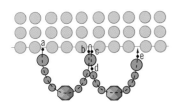

FIGURE 3

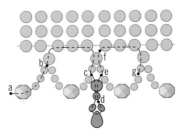

FIGURE 4

Holiday
elegance

by **Celia Martin**

FIGURE 1

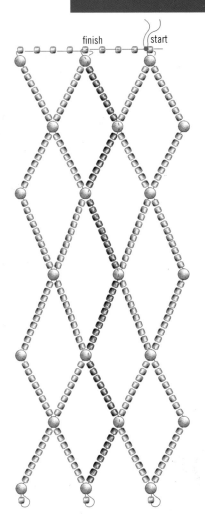

FIGURE 2

Enclosing ornaments and other vessels in a net of beads reminds me of the stained-glass work that my mother does — I love how the light shines through and makes the colors glow. The netting in this ornament is there as a base to work from; it's the canvas. Experimentation with colors and bead types is the fun part.

stepbystep

Netted base

[1] On a comfortable length of thread, pick up 40 10º seed beads, leaving a 6-in. (15cm) tail. Tie the beads into a ring using a surgeon's knot (Basics, p. 6), and sew through the first bead in the ring.

[2] Work the netting as follows:
Row 1: Pick up a 6º seed bead, eight 10ºs, a 6º, eight 10ºs, a 6º, 10 10ºs, a 6º, 10 10ºs, a 6º, eight 10ºs, a 6º, eight 10ºs, a 6º, and a 10º. Turn, skip the 10º, and sew back through the last 6º **(figure 1, a–b)**.
Row 2: Pick up eight 10ºs, a 6º, and eight 10ºs. Skip 17 beads in the previous row, and sew through the next 6º. Pick up 10 10ºs, a 6º, and 10 10ºs. Skip 21 beads in the previous row, and sew through the next 6º. Pick up eight 10ºs, a 6º, and eight 10ºs. Skip 17 beads in the previous row, and sew through the first 6º **(b–c)**.

Sewing left to right, sew through the 10º in the ring above the 6º and the next four 10ºs in the ring **(c–d)**. (There will be three 10ºs between the 10ºs that suspend the netting from the ring.)
Row 3: Pick up a 6º and eight 10ºs. Skip nine beads in the previous row, and sew through the next 6º. Pick up eight 10ºs, a 6º, and 10 10ºs, and sew through the

materials

- round ball ornament, 2½-in. (6.4cm) diameter
- 70 6mm fire-polished beads, round or oval
- hank size 10º seed beads, silver-lined
- 5g size 6º seed beads, silver-lined
- nylon beading thread
- beading needles, #10

6º in the next net. Pick up 10 10ºs, a 6º, and eight 10ºs, and sew through the 6º in the next net. Pick up eight 10ºs, a 6º, and a 10º, skip the 10º, and sew back through the 6º **(d–e)**.
Rows 4–9: Repeat steps 2 and 3 eight times until you have a total of ten 6ºs at the bottom of the netting.
Row 10: To work row 10, which will join row 9 to row 1, pick up eight 10ºs, and sew through the next 6º in row 1. Pick up eight 10ºs, and sew through

41

the next 6º in row 9. Continue joining the rows until you exit the top 6º of row 9 (figure 2, "finish"), then sew through the last three 10ºs in the ring to end at the surgeon's knot with which you originally formed the ring (figure 2, "start"). Tie the working thread and the tail together with a surgeon's knot, and trim the working thread. Do not trim the tail.

[3] Put the netting over an ornament. Add a new thread (Basics) in the beadwork, and exit one of the 10ºs at the bottom of a row (figure 3, point a). Pick up three 10ºs, and sew through the next bottom 10º (a–b). Repeat (b–c) around the bottom of the ornament, forming another 40-bead ring. Sew through all the 10ºs in the ring again without splitting the threads, exiting in the same place you started. Pull the ends to tighten the ring, and tie them together. Do not trim the threads.

Decorative accents

[1] Sew through the 6º above the knot you just tied in the bottom ring. To make the picot, pick up three 10ºs, and sew back through the 6º (figure 4, a–b). To add a dangle, pick up two 10ºs, a 6mm fire-polished bead, and a 10º. Sew back through the 6mm, the two 10ºs, and the 6º (b–c). Sew diagonally through the 10ºs in the netting, making picots and dangles at each 6º all the way to the top (c–d).

[2] Sew left through the 10ºs in the ring, and come out above the next 6º (d–e).

[3] Now work down along the next diagonal line: Sew through the top 6º, pick up two 10ºs, a 6mm, and a 10º. Sew back through the 6mm and two 10ºs and up through the 6º. Pick up three 10ºs, and sew down through the 6º (e–f). Continue down toward the left through the netting, making a dangle and picot at each 6º until you reach the bottom.

[4] After adding the drop at the bottom 6º, sew left through the 10ºs along the bottom ring and start back up the next diagonal as in step 1. Continue up and down until you've added picots and dangles at every intersection.

[5] End all remaining threads (Basics).

FIGURE 3

FIGURE 4

Sparkling spider

by **Diane Hertzler**

These creepy crawlies were originally created to decorate a Christmas tree: in many parts of the world, the legend of the Golden Christmas Spider says that each tree must have a spider to be complete. But this adaptable design would also be a good fit for Halloween decorations. Just paint the wooden beads black, and use coordinating colors for the netting and legs.

a

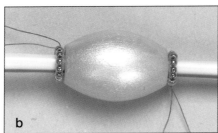

b

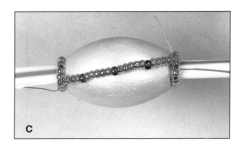

c

step by step

Abdomen

[1] Prime the inside openings of each wooden bead with gesso, and let it dry. Slit a straw lengthwise, slide the beads on the straw, and prime the outside of the beads. Sand until smooth. Paint the inside openings and the outside of each bead with acrylic paint, and let dry.

[2] On 1 yd. (.9m) of beading thread, pick up 12 color A 15º seed beads, leaving a 6-in. (15cm) tail. Sew through the beads again to form a ring. Tie the tail and working thread together with a square knot (Basics, p. 6, and **photo a**).

[3] Leaving a second 6-in. (15cm) tail, cut the ring from the working thread.

[4] Repeat step 2 with the remaining thread on the needle.

[5] Cut a clean straw in half, and slit one piece lengthwise. Slide a bead ring, the oval painted bead, and the other bead ring to the center of the straw **(photo b)**.

[6] To keep track of the top and bottom of the bead as you follow the illustrations, the ring with two tails will be referred to as the bottom ring. With the working thread of the top ring, sew through the next bead.

[7] Work in netting as follows:

Row 1: Pick up a repeating pattern of five As and one color B 15º three times, then pick up five As. Sew through a bead in the bottom ring **(figure 1, a–b** and **photo c)**. The first couple of rows will not fit snugly against the wooden bead, but keep the thread tension tight as you work.

Row 2: Pick up five As, one B, and five As. Sew through the middle B in the previous row **(b–c)**. Pick up five As, one B, and five As, skip a bead in the top ring, and sew through the next bead **(c–d)**.

Row 3: Pick up five As and sew through the first B in the previous row **(d–e)**. Pick up five As, one B, and five As, and sew through the third B in the previous

row **(e–f)**. Pick up five As, skip a bead in the bottom ring, and sew through the next bead **(f–g)**.

Rows 4–11: Repeat rows 2 and 3 four times so there are six Bs around at the top, middle, and bottom of the wooden bead. On the last row, the needle should exit a bead in the bottom ring.

Row 12: To connect row 11 to row 1, pick up five As, and sew through the bottom B in row 1 **(figure 2, a–b)**. Pick up five As, and sew through the middle B in row 11 **(b–c** and **photo d)**. Pick up five As, and sew through the top B in row 1. Pick up five As, and sew through the A in the top ring that row 1 started from **(c–d)**.

[8] Sew through a few more beads in the top ring, keeping the tension tight, and end the thread (Basics) and the remaining tails.

materials

- 1½ x ¾–in. (3.8 x 1.9cm) oval wooden bead
- 10mm round wooden bead
- **72** 5mm bugle beads
- seed beads:
  2g size 11º
  2g size 15º, color A
  1g size 15º, color B
- 3½ ft. (1m) 24-gauge wire
- nylon beading thread
- beading needles, #12
- acrylic paint
- **3** drinking straws
- gesso or primer for acrylic paint
- paint brush
- sandpaper, fine grit
- chainnose pliers
- roundnose pliers
- wire cutters

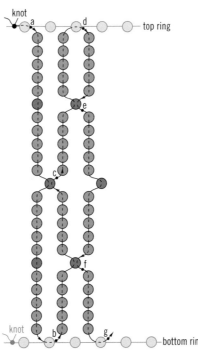

FIGURE 1

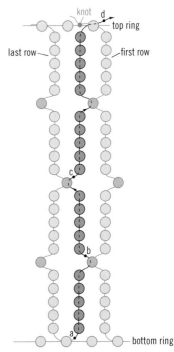

FIGURE 2

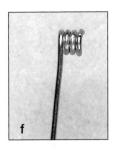

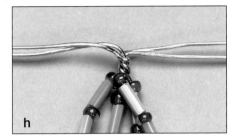

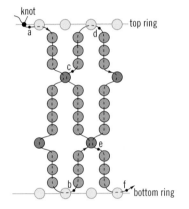

FIGURE 3

FIGURE 4

Head

[1] Repeat steps 2–5 of "Abdomen" using the round wooden bead

[2] Work in netting as follows:

Row 1: Sew through the next bead in the top ring, and pick up three As, one B, four As, one B, and three As. Sew through a bead in the bottom ring (figure 3, a–b).

Row 2: Pick up three As, one B, and four As, and sew through the top B in the previous row (b–c). Pick up three As, skip a bead in the top ring, and sew through the next bead (c–d).

Row 3: Pick up three As, one B, and four As, and sew through the bottom B in the previous row (d–e). Pick up three As, skip a bead in the bottom ring, and sew through the next bead (e–f).

Rows 4–11: Repeat rows 2 and 3 until there are six Bs around the top and the bottom of the wood bead. The thread should exit a bead in the bottom ring.

Row 12: To connect row 11 to row 1, pick up three As, and sew through the bottom

B in row 1 (figure 4, a–b). Pick up four As, and sew through the top B in row 11 (b–c). Pick up three As and sew through the first bead in the top ring (c–d).

[3] End the threads.

Legs

[1] Cut a 5-in. (13cm) piece of wire.

[2] Grasp the very end of the wire with the tip of your roundnose pliers, and wrap the wire around one jaw of the pliers to make a small loop (photo e). Reposition the pliers, and to make two or three more loops next to the first (photo f).

[3] Repeat steps 1 and 2 seven times.

[4] On each wire, string an alternating pattern of an 11º and a bugle until each has 10 11ºs and nine bugles. Start and end with an 11º.

[5] Hold four wires in one hand, making sure the beads on each wire are flush with the coils. With your other hand, twist the wires together directly above the beads. Tighten the twist with chainnose pliers (photo g).

[6] Separate the wires into two pairs, and bend each pair in opposite directions at a right angle to the beaded sections (photo h).

[7] Repeat steps 5 and 6 with the remaining four wires.

[8] Hold both leg sets together with the legs pointing in the same direction. Twist two pairs of perpendicular wires together, and repeat with the other side (photo i). Use chainnose pliers to tighten the twist gently. Be careful not to break any of the wires.

[9] String the beaded abdomen over one of the twisted wire bundles, and trim the wires to ½ in. (1.3cm) past the bead. Treating the twisted wires as one wire, use roundnose pliers to make a loop (photo j). Continue turning the loop until it is snug against the opening of the abdomen bead. The loop should be large enough that is doesn't slide into the bead.

[10] Repeat step 9 with the remaining twisted wire bundle and the head bead.

[11] Shape the legs so they curve up then down over the body of the spider.

[12] Set the spider directly on a surface or tree branch, or thread a ribbon or wire hook (see "Ornament hangers," p. 9) through the loop at the head or tail of the spider's body to hang.

Balloon ornaments

by **Pam O'Connor and Lora Groszkiewicz**

Let your spirits soar as you make this charming hot-air balloon ornament. The balloon is stitched in netting, and the basket can be made in either brick stitch or peyote stitch. Instructions for both baskets are provided, but if you want to put something in the basket, make it with peyote stitch — the brick stitch basket has no bottom!

step by step

If you make the netted top in a single color, ignore bead color references and add together the bead counts between stitches. The netted strips have 36 repeats, but check your first strip to ensure it goes comfortably around the widest part of your ornament, and adjust if needed.

Wide netted strips

[1] On 2 yd. (1.8m) of conditioned thread (Basics, p. 6), attach a stop bead (Basics), leaving a 6-in. (15cm) tail. Make the first strip of netting as follows:

Row 1: Pick up four color A 11º seed beads, three color B 11º seed beads, and an A. Skip the A, and sew back through the last B picked up (**figure 1, a–b**).

Row 2: Pick up two Bs and three As. Sew back through the first A picked up in the previous row (**b–c**). Pick up three Bs and one A. Skip the A, and sew back through the last B (**c–d**).

Row 3: Pick up two Bs and three As. Sew through the center connector bead of the previous five-bead sequence (**d–e**). Pick up three Bs and an A. Skip the A, and sew back through the last B picked up (**e–f**).

Rows 4–71: Repeat rows 2 and 3 (**f–g**) until the chain has 36 points on one side and 35 on the other.

Row 72: After making the 36th point, pick up two Bs and sew through the connector bead in row 1 (**figure 2, a–b**). Pick up two As, and sew through the connector bead in row 71 (**b–c**). Pick up three Bs and an A. Turn and sew back through the next bead (**c–d**). Pick up two Bs, remove the stop bead, and tie the two thread ends together with a square knot (**Basics and d–e**). End the thread (**Basics**).

[2] To make the second wide netted strip, follow the pattern in step 1, but instead of picking up an A at the bottom edge of every other row, sew through a top edge A on the completed strip (**figure 3**).

materials

netted balloon
- round ball ornament, 2½–2¾-in. (6.4–7cm) diameter
- 30g size 11º seed beads, in **1** color, or 15g each of **2** colors: A and B
- nylon beading thread, conditioned with beeswax or Thread Heaven, or Fireline 6 lb. test
- beading needles, #10

peyote stitch basket
- size 11º Japanese cylinder beads: 7g color C 1g color D
- **8** 6mm pressed-glass star beads (optional)

brick stitch basket
- 10g size 8º hex-cut beads
- 1g size 15º seed beads (optional)

[3] Repeat step 2 to add a third netted strip. Repeat again, if desired, to make a fourth netted strip.

Narrow netted strip

Attach a stop bead to 2 yd. (1.8m) of conditioned beading thread, leaving a 6-in. (15cm) tail. Make the narrow netted strip that cinches in the wide strips at the top as follows:

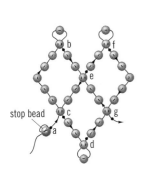

FIGURE 1

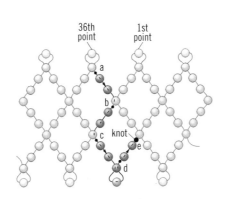

FIGURE 2

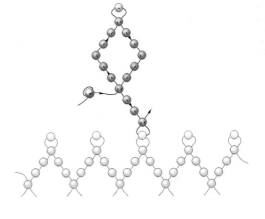

FIGURE 3

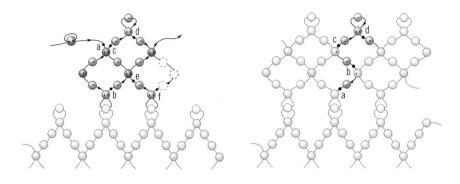

FIGURE 4   FIGURE 5

Row 1: Pick up a B, an A, a B, and two As. Sew through any A on the edge of the wide strip of netting. Turn, and sew back through the next bead (**figure 4, a–b**).

Row 2: Pick up an A, a B, and an A. Go through the top B in the previous row (**b–c**). Pick up two As and a B. Skip the B bead, and sew back through the last A added (**c–d**).

Row 3: Pick up an A, a B, and an A. Sew through the connector bead of the previous three-bead sequence (**d–e**). Pick up two As. Sew through the next A on the wide strip. Turn, and sew back through the next bead (**e–f**).

Rows 4–71: Continue this pattern until you have sewn through the wide strip's last A.

Row 72: To connect row 71 to row 1, pick up an A, and sew through the connector bead in row 1 (**figure 5, a–b**). Pick up an A, and sew through the connector bead in row 71 (**b–c**). Pick up two As and an B. Skip the B, and sew back through the last A added (**c–d**). Pick up an A, remove the stop bead, and tie the working thread and tail with a square knot. Ends the threads.

Netted top

[1] On a 2-yd. (1.8m) length of thread, pick up 36 As, leaving a 6-in. (15cm) tail. Form the beads into a ring, and test to see if the ring fits around the neck of your ornament. If it does not, add the number of beads needed. Divide 36 by the number of extra beads. This number will help you determine where to skip a bead when you're connecting the ring to the netting. For example, if you use 40 beads to make the ring, 36 divided by the four extra beads equals 9, so skip a bead after every nine beads connected.

[2] Tie the tail and working thread with a square knot, leaving about a bead's width of ease. Sew through one or two beads in the ring, pulling the knot into a bead.

[3] Put the netting over the ornament with the narrow netted strip closest to the top and the circle of beads around the ornament's neck.

[4] Pick up 12 As and sew through an A at the top of the narrow netted strip. Sew back through the 12 As and the next bead in the ring (**photo a**).

[5] Repeat step 4 to connect all the A beads on the edge of the netted cover to the ring, skipping beads if needed, as explained in step 1. End the threads.

Peyote stitch basket

[1] On 2 yd. (1.8m) of conditioned thread, pick up 72 color C cylinder beads, leaving a 6-in. (15cm) tail. Tie the beads into a ring with a square knot, leaving two beads' worth of ease. Sew through the first bead.

[2] Work 28 rows of circular, even-count peyote stitch (Basics) with Cs for a total of 30 rows.

[3] Stitch four rows with color D cylinder beads. End the threads.

[4] To start the netted bottom, pick up 12 Cs on 5 ft. (1.5m) of conditioned thread. Tie them into a ring with a square knot, leaving a 6-in. (15cm) tail. Sew through the first bead.

[5] Pick up three Cs, skip a C on the ring, and sew through the next C (**figure 6, a–b**). Repeat around the ring, and sew through the first two Cs of the first three-bead point (**b–c**).

[6] Pick up five Cs, and sew through the center bead of the next three-bead point (**c–d**). Repeat around the ring, and sew through the first three beads of the first five-bead point (**d–e**).

[7] Pick up seven Cs, and sew through the center bead of the next point (**e–f**). Repeat around, and sew through the first four beads of the first seven-bead point (**f–g**).

[8] Pick up nine Cs, and sew through the center bead of the next point (**g–h**). Repeat around the ring.

[9] Sew through the first four beads of the first nine-bead point. Sew through

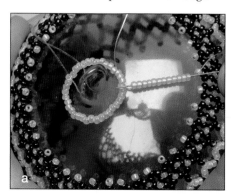

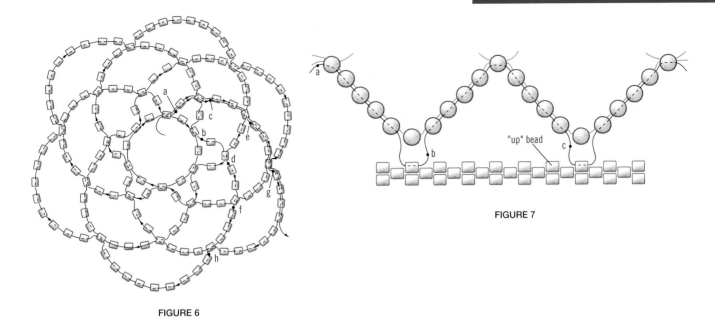

FIGURE 6

FIGURE 7

an up bead on the bottom row of Cs on the basket **(figure 7, a–b)**.

[10] Skip the middle bead on the nine-bead point, and sew through the next nine Cs **(b–c)**.

[11] Skip five up beads on the bottom row of the basket, and sew through the next up bead.

[12] Repeat steps 10 and 11 four times to connect the netted bottom to the basket. End the thread.

Brick stitch basket

[1] On 2 yd. (1.8m) of conditioned thread, pick up two 8º hex-cut beads, leaving a 6-in. (15cm) tail. Sew through both beads again, and tighten so the beads sit side by side. Working in ladder stitch (Basics), pick up a hex-cut, and sew through the previous bead and the new bead. Tighten. Repeat until you have made a ladder of 32 beads.

[2] Connect the ladder into a ring by sewing through the first and last beads again. Tighten.

[3] Pick up two hex-cuts, sew under the thread bridge between the next two beads in the ring, and sew back through the second bead picked up. Continue in brick stitch (Basics) to complete the round.

[4] Repeat step 3 seven times to complete nine rows of beadwork. End the thread.

Ornament assembly

[1] Add a new 2-yd. (1.8m) thread to the basket, exiting a bead in the top round (an up bead if you made the peyote basket).

[2] Pick up 50 As and sew through an A on the bottom edge of the netting **(photo b)**. Sew back through the 50 As, and tighten.

[3] Count over nine up beads on the peyote basket or eight beads on the brick stitch basket. Sew through the beadwork to exit this bead.

[4] Repeat step 2, counting over nine As on the netted edge to determine the next bead you'll sew through.

[5] Repeat steps 2–4 twice to connect the basket to the netting. End the threads.

Embellishment

The red-and-gold ornament features two fringes with pressed-glass star beads at each connecting point on the basket. The ornament with the cream-colored brick stitch basket has beaded "swags" added around the top (using 15º beads). You could also try embellishing the connecting strands with picot stitches or adding dagger beads at the bottom edge of the netting.

b

Ornaments take wing

by **Deb Moffett-Hall**

For this project, I set out to design a different kind of beaded ornament with peyote stitch panels to depict scenes. It takes 132 Japanese cylinder beads to go around the ornament slightly above the widest circumference. Because I prefer to do flat even-count peyote stitch, making six panels was the answer. To achieve a tapestry effect, I graphed the panels with pointed bottoms and accented each point with a beaded tassel. There are practical advantages to this design, which has a netted top and an open bottom — if the ornament breaks, you simply drape the beadwork over another ornament.

step by step

Bird panels

[1] Attach a stop bead (Basics, p. 6) to 2 yd. (1.8m) of conditioned thread (Basics), leaving a 6-in. (15cm) tail. Pick up 22 color A cylinder beads, and, working in flat, even-count peyote stitch (Basics), weave a cardinal panel (see patterns, p. 53) until you reach the row before the first decrease for the tapered point.

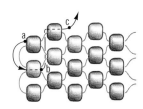

FIGURE 1

[2] You will need to reposition your thread before stitching a decrease row so that the thread will not show: Sew through the bead directly below the last bead sewn through, pointing toward the panel (figure 1, a–b).
[3] Sew between the last bead on the next-to-last row and the last bead added, passing under the thread that connects them. Tug gently to reposition the thread, and sew back through the last bead added (b–c). This puts your thread in position to start the first decrease row.
[4] Repeat steps 2 and 3 at the end of every row in the point. After you add the last bead, sew back up into the panel, and end the thread (Basics). Remove the stop bead, and end the tail.
[5] Work as in steps 1–4 to stitch three cardinal and three chickadee panels.

Tassels

[1] Attach a stop bead on 4 ft. (1.2m) of conditioned thread, leaving a 6-in. (15cm) tail. Pick up a color C cylinder, two color B cylinders, a C, a B, a C, a bugle bead, a C, a B, an A, a B, a C, a bugle, a C, a B, an 11º seed bead, an 8mm heart bead, an 11º seed bead, a 6mm bicone bead, and an 11º (figure 2). Skip the last 11º seed bead, and sew back through all the fringe beads.
[2] Skip the top C, and sew back through the next two Bs and one C. String another fringe, but begin the pattern at the second pair of Bs. Skip the end 11º, and sew back through all the fringe beads, including the three at the top of the first fringe.
[3] Repeat step 2 twice. Set the four-fringe tassel aside without ending the threads.
[4] Repeat steps 1–3 11 times to create a total of 12 tassels.
[5] Remove the stop beads from two tassels. Sew the four thread tails (two from each tassel) through a 4mm blue bicone bead and a 3mm round gold bead.
[6] Divide the threads into two groups of two threads each. Sew two threads through the point bead on a panel in one direction and the other two threads through the point bead in the opposite direction. Pull the threads to snug the tassel up to the panel.
[7] One by one, sew each tail into the beadwork and end the thread.
[8] Repeat steps 5–7, attaching a double tassel to each of the five remaining panels.

Joining the panels

[1] Alternating the cardinal and chickadee panels, position the panels face up in a circle with the points to the outside. Be sure that an up bead is the first bead on the top left and a down bead is on the top right of each panel.
[2] Start a new 2-yd. (1.8m) thread in one of the panels, exiting the top right-hand bead (the low bead). Pick up a color C cylinder, and sew through the next A (photo a) to begin a row of peyote stitch with Cs.

materials

- round ball ornament, 2¼-in. (5.7cm) diameter
- **48** 8mm glass heart-shaped beads, frosted blue
- **48** 6mm glass bicone beads, frosted white
- **6** 4mm bicone beads, blue
- **6** 3mm round beads, gold
- **30g** 6–9mm bugle beads
- **144** size 11º seed beads, gold
- size 11º Japanese cylinder beads:
  11g matte opalescent light sapphire (#760), color A
  6g white pearl (#201), color B
  5g bright metal gold (#411), color C
  2g dyed matte opalescent olive (#797), color D
  2g dyed opalescent cranberry (#654), color E
  2g matte metallic teal iris (#327), color F
  1g black (#010), color G
  1g ceylon beige (#205), color H
  1g dyed matte opalescent sienna (#794), color I
  1g opalescent chocolate (#734), color J
  1g opalescent light red (#791), color K
  12 opalescent yellow (#160), color L
- nylon beading thread, conditioned with beeswax or Thread Heaven
- beading needles, #12

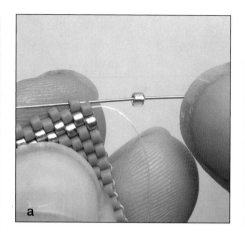

a

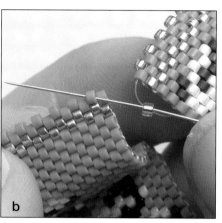

b

[3] When you reach the end of the panel, pick up a C and sew through the second top right bead (an up bead) of the next panel (**photo b**). Secure the join by sewing down into the panel a few beads and back across to the first panel. Zigzag through a few rows and sew back across. End by coming out the second top right bead to continue with the row of peyote stitch across the top of the second panel.

[4] Repeat step 3 to connect the four remaining panels. To join the panels into a ring, at the end of the sixth panel, pick up a C, and sew through the top right C on the first panel. Work a second round of peyote stitch with Cs to lock the panels together. Do not end the thread.

Netted top

To make the netting, the panels must be draped over an ornament. You may want to use an old ornament as you work the netting because the needle may scratch the surface. The key to creating well-fitted netting is to hold the peyote panels snugly over the ornament so you do not pull the netting threads too tight as you work. Begin with the thread exiting the top left up bead of a chickadee panel.

[1] Pick up a repeating pattern of one C, one B, one C, and a bugle two times, then pick up one C, one B, and one C.

[2] Skip the next four up beads, and sew through the following up bead (figure 3, a–b). Pick up one C and sew through the next up bead (b–c).

[3] Pick up the same pattern of beads as in step 1.

[4] Skip the next four up beads, and sew through the following up bead (c–d).

[5] Repeat steps 1–4 five times, adding a C at every other connection of the netting so that you are adding a C at the center of each panel.

[6] To get into position for the second round of netting, sew through the first six beads in the first loop of the first row of netting (e–f).

[7] Continue in netting as follows:
Round 2: Pick up one C, two Bs, one C, two Bs, and one C. Sew through the middle B on the next loop in the previous round (f–g). Repeat around, then sew through the first four beads in the first loop of the round (h–i).
Round 3: Pick up two Bs, one C, and two Bs. Sew through the middle C on the next loop in the previous round (i–j). Repeat around, then sew through the first three beads in the first loop of the round (k–l).
Round 4: Repeat round 3 (l–m).
Round 5: Pick up three Bs, and sew through the middle C of the next loop in the previous round (m–n). Repeat around. This is the last round of netting and will encircle the top of the ornament. Sew through all the beads in round 5 again, and tighten to secure the top of the ornament cover.

[8] Sew back through the netting, and end the thread in a peyote panel.

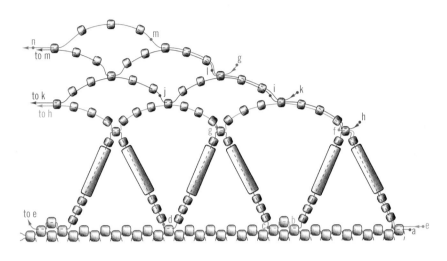

FIGURE 3

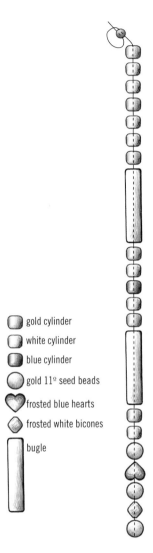

gold cylinder

white cylinder

blue cylinder

gold 11º seed beads

frosted blue hearts

frosted white bicones

bugle

FIGURE 2

Victorian swags ornament

by **Jane Jayne**

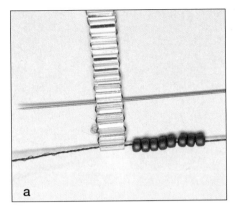

a

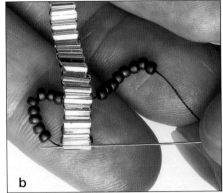

b

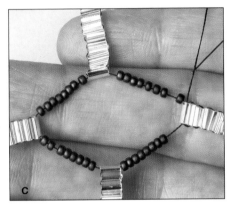

c

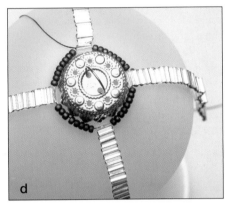

d

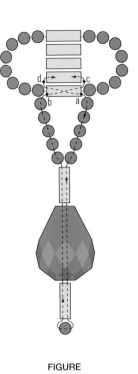

FIGURE

In 1999, my friend Caroline Head took me to a beading class. That year for Christmas, she gave me a beautiful ornament she made using a beading pattern from *Bead&Button* magazine. The following Christmas, she gave me another ornament, and soon after, I made my first trip to the local bead shop. I love to see bugle beads draped and woven through seed beads. From that vision, this pattern emerged.

step by step

Bugle ladders
[1] With 1 yd. (.9m) of conditioned thread (Basics, p. 6), work in ladder stitch (Basics) to make a ladder with bugle beads that is 40 beads long.
[2] Reinforce the ladder by sewing back through the bugles. Don't cut the thread.
[3] Repeat steps 1 and 2 to complete a total of four ladders.

Ladder decoration
[1] With the working end of the thread on one ladder, pick up eight 11° seed beads, and sew through the fifth bugle from the bottom of the ladder (photo a). Pick up eight 11°s, and sew through the last bugle in the ladder to make a loop on the other side (photo b). Pull tight.

[2] Pick up five 11°s, a bugle, a teardrop bead, a bugle, and an 11°. Sew back through the bugle, the drop, and the bugle. Pick up five 11°s (figure, a–b), and sew through the last bugle on the ladder. Weave both ends of the thread through several bugles (b–c and a–d) in the ladder to secure it.
[3] Repeat steps 1 and 2 for each ladder.

Join the ladders
[1] Add a new 1-yd. (.9m) thread in one of the ladders, leaving a 4-in. (10cm) tail. Exit the top bugle, and pick up eight 11°s. Sew through the top bugle in the next ladder, and pick up eight more 11°s. Repeat until all four ladders and 32 11°s are strung.

materials
- round ball ornament, 2½-in. (6.4cm) diameter
- 4 16 x 8mm teardrop beads
- 14g 5mm bugle beads
- hank size 11° seed beads
- 4–5g size 11° Charlottes, gold or silver
- nylon beading thread, conditioned with beeswax or Thread Heaven
- beading needles, #12
- glue

EDITOR'S NOTE:
As you work, you may want to place the glass ornament on a short candlestick, cup, or mug to give it some stability.

[2] Sew through the top bugle on the first ladder again to form a circle (photo c). Sew through all the beads again for security. Put the beadwork over the top of a glass ornament (photo d). Tie the working thread and tail with a surgeon's knot (Basics). Dab the knot with glue and end the thread (Basics).

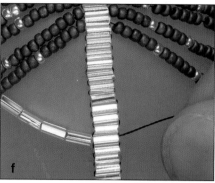

Seed bead swags

String all the seed bead swags, moving from left to right around the ornament. To add extra sparkle, mix a few gold or silver Charlottes with the main color seed beads, adding them randomly throughout the swags.

[1] Add a new 1½-yd. (1.4m) thread to one of the ladders, and exit the second bugle from the top.

[2] Pick up 38 11°s, and sew through the 20th bugle from the top of the second ladder (photo e).

[3] Pick up 38 11°s, and sew through the second bugle from the top of the third ladder. Repeat step 2 with the fourth ladder.

[4] Repeat step 3, but sew through the third bugle of the first ladder to begin the next round.

[5] Pick up 40 11°s, and sew through the 21st bugle from the top of the second ladder.

[6] Pick up 40 11°s, and sew through the third bugle from the top of the third ladder.

[7] Repeat steps 5 and 6, but sew through the fourth bugle of the first ladder.

Bugle bead swags

String the bugle bead swags, moving from left to right as you move around the ornament. The bugle swags alternately pass over and under the seed swags. (In the green-and-silver version below, all the bugle swags pass over the seed swags.)

[1] Add a new 1½-yd. (1.4m) thread to the second ladder, exiting the second bugle from the top.

[2] Pick up 12 bugles, and sew through the 20th bead from the top of the third ladder (photo f).

[3] Pick up 12 bugles, and slide the needle underneath the 10 rows of seed beads, being careful not to catch the seed beads. Sew through the second bugle from the top of the fourth ladder (photo g).

[4] Pick up 12 bugles, and sew through the 20th bugle from the top of the first ladder. Pick up 12 bugles, and slide the needle under the 10 rows of 11°s. Sew through the third bugle from the top of the ladder from which you started the round.

[5] For the second row, pick up 13 bugles, and pass them over the 11°s. Work in the same manner as for the seed bead swags, adding one more bugle to each section of each round. Work a total of six rounds. The final round will have 17 bugles in each section. When you finish the last swag of bugles, end the threads.

Other
Stitching

Add a little color

by **Diane Hertzler**

Remember how exciting it was as a child to open a new box of crayons? Here's one made in herringbone stitch over a wooden dowel that will always stay new! You can personalize this crayon ornament by stitching the date into the wrapper.

step by step

Crayon

[1] Sharpen a dowel to a blunt point and paint it with two coats of paint, allowing time to dry between coats. Finish both ends with a coat of varnish.

[2] On a comfortable length of beading thread, pick up 28 color B cylinder beads, leaving a 6-in. (15cm) tail.

[3] Create a bead ladder (Basics, p. 6) two beads high and 14 sets long. Form the ladder into a ring by sewing through the two end sets. Hold the ring with the tail exiting the bottom and the working thread exiting the same set of beads on the top. Slide the ring over the dowel with the point facing down.

[4] Pick up two color A cylinders, and sew down through the next set of beads (figure 1, a–b). Sew up through the next set of beads, pick up two As, and sew down through the next set of beads (b–c). Continue around (c–d). Step up by sewing through two beads in the ladder and the first bead added in this round (d–e).

[5] Work 48 rounds of tubular herringbone stitch (Basics), following figure 2 to determine color changes.

[6] Work round 51 in tubular herringbone, but pick up four Bs in each stitch rather than two, and exit the bead shown (figure 3, a–b). Reverse direction, and sew

up through three beads and down through two beads (b–c). Pull snug. Sew up through two beads and down through two (c–d).

[7] Repeat around to create the look of a ladder at the top of the crayon (d–e). Reverse direction, and sew up through two beads (e–f).

Hanging loop

[1] Sew through the beadwork to exit the bead shown (figure 4, a–b).

[2] Pick up 10 As, skip seven beads, and sew down through the top two Bs in the next column (b–c).

[3] Sew up through the two adjacent beads and back through the beads in the loop. Skip five beads, and sew down through the top two beads in the next column (c–d). Sew up through the next two beads (d–e).

[4] Retrace the thread path through the loop to reinforce it, and end the threads (Basics). Thread ribbon or wire hook (see "Ornament hangers," p. 9) through the loop to hang the crayon.

materials:

- size 11º cylinder beads:
  2.5g color A, yellow AB
  1.5g color B, yellow opaque
  2g color C, black
- nylon beading thread, size B, yellow
- #10 beading needles
- 3½ in. (8.9cm) dowel, ¼ in. (6mm) diameter
- acrylic paint, yellow
- artist acrylic paintbrush, approx. size 4
- handheld pencil sharpener
- water-based varnish, satin finish

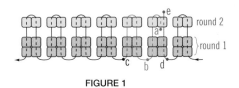

FIGURE 1

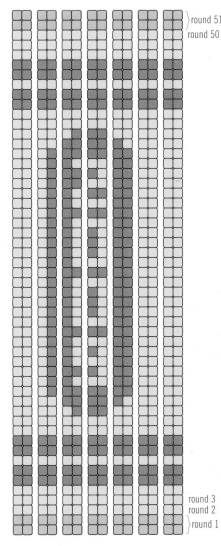

FIGURE 2

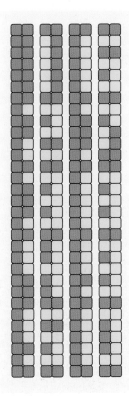

All numbers have been graphed here so the crayon can be personalized with any date.

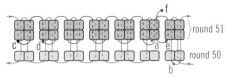

FIGURE 3

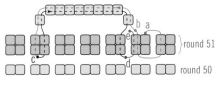

FIGURE 4

Miniature moccasin

by **Diane Hertzler**

While visiting a Native American museum, I was impressed with the handcrafted moccasins that were on display. They ranged in size from infant to adult, and the attention to detail was evident on every pair. I have always been drawn to the Southwest, so I selected bead colors for my miniature moccasin to remind me of my trip to the area.

materials

- size 11º seed beads:
  3.5g color A, mustard
  1g color B, dark rust
  1g color C, coral
  0.5g color D, dark turquoise
  0.5g color E, light turquoise
- nylon beading thread, size B, gold
- beading needles, #10 or #12
- 3 x 12 in. (7.6 x 30cm) piece of suede or Ultrasuede, tan
- 3 x 3 in. (7.6 x 7.6cm) piece of tracing paper
- magnetic board (optional)
- rotary cutter and mat (optional)
- scissors
- soft lead pencil

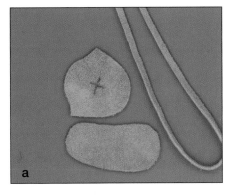

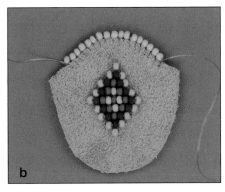

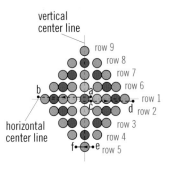

FIGURE 1A

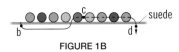

FIGURE 1B

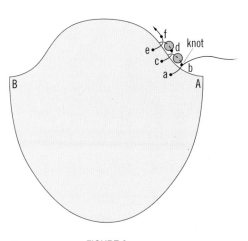

FIGURE 2

stepbystep

Prepare the suede

[1] Using scissors or a rotary cutter and mat, cut a ⅛ x 12-in. (3 x 300mm) strip from the long side of a piece of suede for the shoelace.

[2] Transfer the **toe** and **sole patterns**, p. 62, onto tracing paper, and cut them out. With a pencil, trace the patterns onto the suede. Cut the toe and sole from the suede, and mark the center of the toe piece with horizontal and vertical lines **(photo a)**.

Toe bead embroidery

[1] Thread a needle with a comfortable length of thread. Knot the end, and work with a single strand. Embroider the toe as follows:

Row 1: Sew up through the suede half an 11º seed bead's width to the right of center on the horizontal line **(figure 1A, point a)**. Pick up a color B, a color A, a color E, a color D, and a color C 11º seed bead. Move the beads down the thread to lie on the horizontal line. Sew down through the suede on the horizontal line right next to the last bead strung, and pull snug **(a–b)**.

Sew up through the suede between the A and the B. Sew through the B **(figure 1B, b–c)**. Pick up an A, an E, a D, and a C. Move the beads down the thread to lie on the horizontal line. Sew down through the suede on the horizontal line right next to the last bead, and pull snug **(figure 1A, c–d and figure 1B, c–d)**.

Rows 2–4: Repeat row 1, decreasing the number of beads in each row by two (row 2 should have seven beads, row 3 should have five beads, row 4 should have three beads). The center beads

should lie on the vertical line below the B **(figure 1A)**.

Row 5: Sew up through the suede half an 11º's width to the right of the center line, and pick up a C. Move the bead down the thread to position it on the vertical line. Sew down through the suede right next to the bead, and pull snug **(figure 1A, e–f)**.

Rows 6–9: Repeat rows 2–5, making the top half of the diamond design the mirror image of the bottom half.

[2] End the thread: On the underside of the suede, sew under a thread and tie a half-hitch knot (Basics, p. 6). Repeat, and trim close to the work.

Edge stitching

By adding beads to a buttonhole stitch, this edging will be used to finish the raw edge of the suede along the tongue, sew the toe to the sole, and provide a base from which to begin peyote stitch.

Tongue

[1] Thread a needle with a comfortable length of thread. Work on a single strand with no knot.

[2] Sew up through the suede ⅛ in. (3mm) from the edge **(figure 2, point a)**. Leaving a 6-in. (15cm) tail, tie the working thread and tail with a square knot (Basics). The knot should lie on the edge of the suede.

[3] Pick up an A, and sew up through to the right side of the suede ⅛ in. (3mm) from the edge and one bead's width to the left of the first stitch **(b–c)**.

[4] Sew through the thread loop that formed to the left side of the bead **(c–d)**. Pull snug.

[5] Pick up an A, and sew through to the right side of the suede ⅛ in. (3mm) from the edge and one bead's width to the left of the previous stitch **(d–e)**.

[6] Repeat step 4 (e–f). Pull snug. The beads should sit side by side along the edge of the suede.

[7] Repeat steps 5 and 6 to add As between points A and B of the toe pattern **(photo b)**.

[8] To end the thread, tie a half hitch knot under the last loop, and sew between several beads and the edge of the suede. Trim close to the work. Thread a needle on the tail, and repeat.

Toe and sole attachment

[1] Thread a needle with a comfortable length of thread. Work on a single strand with no knot.

[2] Place the toe on top of the sole, undersides together, matching points C on both patterns. Sew through both

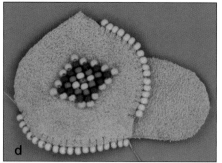

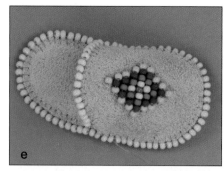

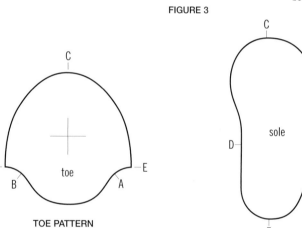

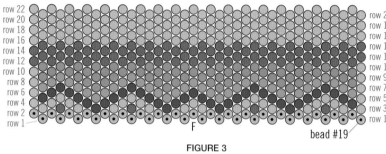

row 22 row 21
row 20 row 19
row 18 row 17
row 16 row 15
row 14 row 13
row 12 row 11
row 10 row 9
row 8   row 7
row 6   row 5
row 4   row 3
row 2   row 1
row 1

F

bead #19

FIGURE 3

C

D — | — E

B   A

toe

TOE PATTERN

C

D — sole — E

F

SOLE PATTERN

Finishing

[1] Fold the peyote work to the outside of the moccasin between rows 15 and 16, forming a cuff. Center the shoelace under the cuff.

[2] Zip (Basics) the cuff in place by sewing row 22 to row 11 (photo f). Tie a half-hitch knot. Sew through the cuff to exit the center bead in row 18.

[3] Pick up nine As, and sew through the center bead in row 21. Pull snug, forming a loop on the back of the moccasin from which to hang the ornament.

[4] Retrace the thread path through the loop a few times, and end the thread. Thread a ribbon or wire hook (see "Ornament hangers," p. 9) through the loop to hang the moccasin.

[5] Tie the shoelace into a bow, and trim the ends to the desired length.

DESIGNER'S TIP:
Try placing your graph on a magnetic board with a straight edge or ruler. This will help you easily maintain your place in the pattern.

---

pieces of suede at point C from the bottom of the sole through the top of the toe, ⅛ in. (3mm) from the edge. Leave an 18-in. (46cm) tail, and tie the thread with a square knot (photo c).

[3] Work edge stitch as described in steps 3–6 of "Tongue" through both pieces of suede from point C to D on the patterns. It will be necessary to adjust the upper piece of suede as the two pieces are sewn together to keep both edges even (photo d).

[4] Continue around the sole, adding edge stitch between points D to E. Do not cut the thread.

[5] Thread a needle on the tail, and work edge stitch through both pieces of suede from point C to E. As you work down this side of the toe, you will sew through the loop that forms to the right

side of the bead. Again, it will be necessary to move the upper piece of suede as the pieces are sewn together. End the thread.

Peyote sides, back, and cuff

The edge-stitched beads on the sides and back of the sole will be used as rows 1 and 2 of the peyote stitch section. These beads are marked with a • on figure 3.

[1] Locate the center back bead on the sole (F) and count 19 beads to the right. With the thread that is left from the toe attachment, sew through the beadwork to exit that bead (figure 3 and photo e).

[2] Following the pattern in figure 3, work in flat, even-count peyote stitch (Basics) to complete rows 3–22.

Flurries in the forecast

by **Linda Joy Mitchell**

Silver-lined beads and crystals make these snowflakes glisten. Hang ornaments in a window for a delightful holiday decoration or tie individual snowflakes onto presents to add a special touch.

step by step

[1] On 1 yd. (.9m) of conditioned beading thread (Basics, p. 6), pick up eight 11º seed beads, leaving an 8-in. (20cm) tail. Sew through the first bead again to form a ring **(figure 1, a–b).**

[2] Pick up a cylinder bead, a bugle bead, a color A 4mm crystal, and three 11ºs. Sew back through the A, bugle, and cylinder **(b–c).**

[3] Sew through the next bead on the ring **(c–d),** and repeat step 2. Continue around the ring to make a total of eight points.

[4] Sew through the points and the center ring again to reinforce them. Exit any bead in the center ring.

[5] Pick up an 11º, a color B 4mm crystal, and an 11º. Skip four beads on the ring, and sew through the next four beads, so you exit the bead where you started. Sew through the 11ºs and B just added and the other half of the ring **(figure 2).** Repeat to add a B on the other side of the snowflake.

[6] Position the working thread so it exits the ring next to the tail. Tie the tail and working thread together with a square knot (Basics). End the threads (Basics).

[7] Repeat steps 1–6 six times to make a total of seven snowflakes.

[8] Remove the metal cap from an ornament. If the cap doesn't have a circle of holes, remove the wire loop,

materials

- round ball ornament, 3-in. (7.6cm) diameter
- 4mm bicone crystals:
  56 color A
  21 color B
- **56** bugle beads, size 2
- **1g** size 11º Japanese cylinder beads
- **3g** size 11º seed beads
- nylon beading thread to match bead color, conditioned with beeswax, or Fireline 6 lb. test
- beading needles, #12
- awl or metal punch (optional)
- Future floor polish (optional)

place the cap face down on a padded surface, and use an awl or metal punch to make seven holes in the cap **(figure 3).**

[9] Add 1 yd. (.9m) of thread (Basics) in a snowflake, and exit the center bead

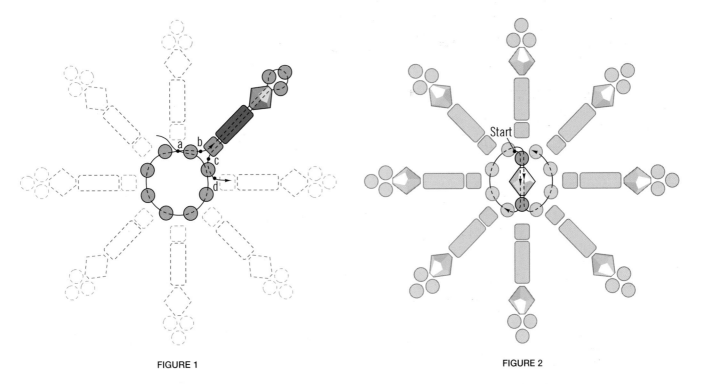

FIGURE 1

FIGURE 2

FIGURE 3

FIGURE 4

EDITOR'S NOTE:
Use floor polish to stiffen and shape the snowflakes. Use a small brush to lightly apply the floor polish to each snowflake before attaching it to the cap. Don't saturate the snowflakes; they need to bend slightly to fit inside the ornament.

at the end of a point. Pick up nine 11ºs, a B, and 12 11ºs, and sew through a hole in the ornament's cap.

[10] Pick up four 11ºs, and sew down through the next hole in the cap. Pick up nine 11ºs, a B, and 12 11ºs. Sew through the center bead in another snowflake's point and back through the beads just strung. Sew through a hole in the cap, pick up four 11ºs, and sew down through the next hole **(figure 4)**. Attach the remaining snowflakes with the following bead counts:
3rd: seven 11ºs, B, seven 11ºs
4th: eight 11ºs, B, seven 11ºs

5th: 16 11ºs, B, one 11º
6th: six 11ºs, B, eight 11ºs
7th: 12 11ºs, B, 11 11ºs.

[11] Reinforce the beads on the top of the cap with a second thread path. Then secure the threads, and trim.

[12] Gently insert the snowflake dangles into the glass ornament, one at a time, and attach the cap. Thread a ribbon or wire hook (see "Ornament hangers," p. 9) through the loop on the cap to hang the ornament.

Pretty plumage

by **Diane Hertzler**

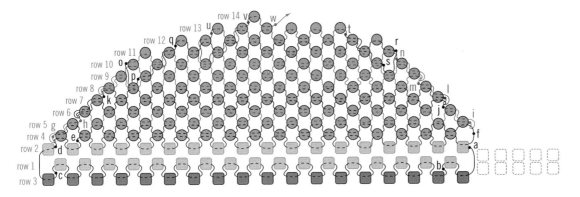

FIGURE 1

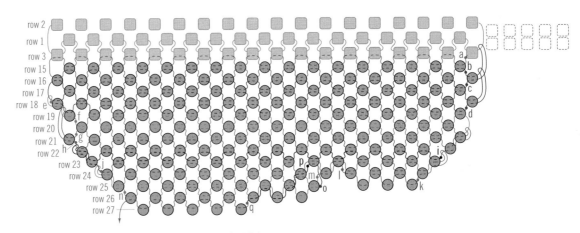

FIGURE 2

Deck your house with peyote stitch feathers. You can vary the pattern of your design to represent the feathers of any domestic or exotic birds.

stepbystep

Body

[1] Stitch the body of the feather in peyote stitch (Basics, p. 6) as follows:

Rows 1 and **2:** Attach a stop bead (Basics) to a comfortable length of thread. Pick up 35 11º cylinder beads, leaving a 6-in. (15cm) tail.

Row 3: Pick up one cylinder, skip the previous cylinder (**figure 1, a–b**), and sew through the next. Continue working in peyote stitch across the row (**b–c**). To turn, pick up a cylinder, and sew through the first bead in row 2 **(c–d)**.

Row 4: Row 4 will be sewn to row 2 rather than row 3: Pick up a color B 11º seed bead, and sew through the next cylinder in row 2 **(d–e)**. Work peyote stitch across the row, following the color pattern shown in **(e–f)**.

Row 5: Work the row and exit at **point g**. To turn, sew under the thread bridge between the bead exited and the bead that sits diagonally below it. Sew back through the bead exited and the last bead added **(g–h)**.

Row 6: Work the row, and exit at **point i**. To turn, sew under the thread bridge between the bead exited and the bead below it. Sew back through the bead exited and the last bead added **(i–j)**.

Row 7: Work the row, and repeat the turn shown at the end of row 5 **(j–k)**.

Row 8: Work the row, and exit at **point l**. Repeat the turn shown at the end of row 5 **(l–m)**.

Rows 9 and **10:** Work each row, turning as in row 5 **(m–n)**.

Row 11: Work the row, and exit at **point o**. To turn, sew through the bead below the one exited **(o–p)**. Sew through three beads that sit at an angle **(p–q)**.

Row 12: Work the row, and exit at **point r**. To turn, sew through the bead below the one exited **(r–s)**. Sew through the three beads that sit at an angle **(s–t)**.

materials
- 0.5g size 11º cylinder beads, natural
- size 11º seed beads:
  2g color A, natural
  2.5g color B, rust
- nylon beading thread, size B, natural
- beading needles, #10
- size 12 snap swivel, with the snap removed
- magnetic board (optional)
- wire cutters (optional)

FIGURE 3

Row 13: Work the row (t–u), and repeat the turn at the end of row 11 (u–v).
Row 14: Pick up one bead, and sew through the next (v–w). Sew through the beadwork to exit at **figure 2, point a.**
Rows 15 and **16:** Work the rows and exit the bead shown (a–b). Pick up one 11º. To turn, sew under the thread bridge between the two beads above it. Sew through the last bead added (b–c).
Rows 17 and **18:** Work the rows, and repeat the turn at the end of row 16 (c–d).
Row 19: Work the row, and exit the bead shown (d–e). To turn, sew under the thread bridge between the two beads above the bead exited and back through the bead exited and the last bead added (e–f).
Rows 20 and **21:** Work the rows, and exit the bead shown (f–g). Pick up one bead, and sew under the thread bridge between the bead above it and the one diagonally above it. Sew back through the bead just added (g–h).
Row 22: Work the row. To turn, sew under the thread bridge between the bead just exited and the one that sits above it. Sew back through the bead just exited and the last bead added (h–i).
Row 23: Work the row. To turn, sew under the thread bridge between the

bead just exited and the one that sits diagonally above it. Sew back through the bead just exited and the last bead strung (i–j).
Row 24: Work the row, and repeat the turn at the end of row 23 (j–k).
Row 25: Work three stitches (k–l). Sew through the bead diagonally above, and exit the next bead in row 24 (l–m). Work to the end of the row, and repeat the turn at the end of row 23 (m–n).
Row 26: Work eight stitches (n–o). To turn, sew through the bead above the bead just exited (o–p). Follow the thread path, and sew to exit the bead shown (p–q).
Row 27: Work across the row.
[2] End the thread (Basics).

Spine ends
Top
Thread a needle with the tail end of the thread. Pick up one cylinder, and sew through the end bead in row 3 (**figure 3, a–b**). End the thread.

Base
[1] Add a new thread (Basics) in the beadwork, and exit at **point c.** Pick up two cylinders, and sew through the end bead in row 2 (c–d). Sew through the

adjacent cylinder and the first cylinder added in this step (d–e).
[2] Repeat to the desired length, and exit at **point f.**
[3] Pick up three cylinders and the loop on a snap swivel. Sew through the two end beads (f–g). Retrace the thread path through the loop to reinforce the connection. If the swivel has a snap attached, remove it by cutting it with the wire cutters.
[4] Create an S-hook or embellished S-hook ornament hanger (see "Ornament hangers," p. 9); however, do not wrap the second eye on the hook until it has been threaded through the other end of the swivel loop. Make the final eye.

EDITOR'S NOTES:
• It is important to maintain a snug tension throughout the project to achieve the shape of the feather.
• Place the graph on a magnetic board with a straight edge or ruler. This will enable you to easily maintain your place in the pattern.

Pumpkin patch

by **Diane Hertzler**

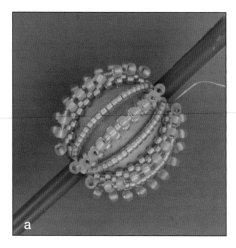

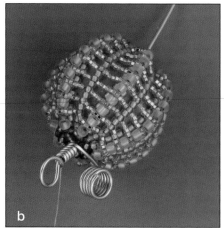

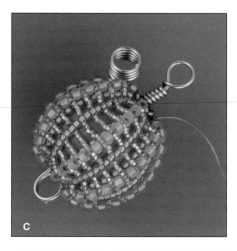

Autumn has always been my favorite time of year, and pumpkins are a symbol of this beautiful season of color, harvest, and refreshing cool breezes. Use this pumpkin with its tubular herringbone stem and simple wirework embellishments to bring autumn's bounty inside the house.

step by step

Prepare the wooden bead

[1] Paint a wooden bead with one coat of primer or gesso. Let it dry, and lightly sand it if needed. Follow with two coats of acrylic paint, allowing time to dry between coats.

[2] On a comfortable length of thread, pick up 14 color A 11° seed beads, leaving a 6-in. (15cm) tail. Sew through the beads again, and pull snug to form a ring of beads. Tie the working thread and the tail with a square knot (Basics, p. 6).

[3] End the thread and the tail (Basics). Repeat to create the second ring; however, do not end the working thread.

[4] Cut a drinking straw in half and slit it lengthwise. Insert it into the wooden bead. Slide each ring of beads over opposite ends of the straw to rest at each end of the wooden bead. The ring with the working thread should be placed at the top of the wooden bead. Sew through the bead next to the knot.

Spokes

Fourteen spokes, to be called "simple" and "complex spokes," will be created between the two rings of beads.

[1] To make a simple spoke, pick up 21 A 11°s, and sew through an A 11° in the bottom ring (**figure 1, a–b**).

[2] Sew back through the 21 beads (**b–c**). Sew through the first bead exited and the next bead in the top ring (**c–d**).

[3] To make a complex spoke, pick up 21 A 11°s, and sew through the next bead on the bottom ring and the last bead picked up (**d–e**).

[4] Using A 11°s, work in flat even-count peyote stitch (Basics) to the top of the spoke (**figure 2, a–b**).

[5] Sew through the bead in the top ring and the first bead in the spoke (**b–c**).

[6] Pick up a color A 8° seed bead, and sew through the next bead in the center row of the spoke (**figure 3, a–b**).

[7] Repeat step 6, adding nine more A 8°s (**b–c**).

[8] Sew through the bead in the bottom ring and the next bead on the bottom ring (**c–d**).

[9] Repeat steps 1–8 six times to add 12 more spokes around the wooden bead in an alternating pattern of simple and complex (**photo a**).

Horizontal rounds

Each round will be connected to the simple spokes and will rest between the 8°s on the complex spokes to create the look of rounded ribs on the pumpkin. Each horizontal round will be sewn through two times to "tweak" the round into position. (**Figure 4** does not show all of the spokes on the bead.)

materials
- 25mm wooden bead, 5.6mm hole
- seed beads
  5g size 11°, color A, orange
  3g size 8°, color A, orange
  2g size 14°, color A, orange
  0.25g size 11°, color B, green
  0.25g size 14°, color B, green
  0.25g size 14°, color C, brown
- 15 in. (38cm) 18-gauge craft wire
- nylon beading thread, size B, orange
- beading needles, #12
- acrylic paint to match orange beads
- artist's acrylic paintbrush, approx. size 4
- drinking straw
- water-based primer or gesso
- sandpaper, fine grit
- flatnose pliers
- roundnose pliers
- wire cutters

Round 1: Sew through the beadwork to exit the third A 11° in a simple spoke (**figure 4, point a**). Pick up eight color A 14° seed beads, and sew through the third A 11° in the next simple spoke (**a–b**). Repeat around the bead, connecting each simple spoke with a horizontal string of beads. After completing the round, sew through each set of horizontal beads again, sewing through the spoke bead in the opposite direction than in the first round (**c–d**).

Round 2: When you get back to the first spoke, sew through the next two A 11°s (**d–e**). Work as in round 1, but pick up nine A 14°s per stitch.

Rounds 3–9: Continue working rounds as in round 1, adding one A 14° per

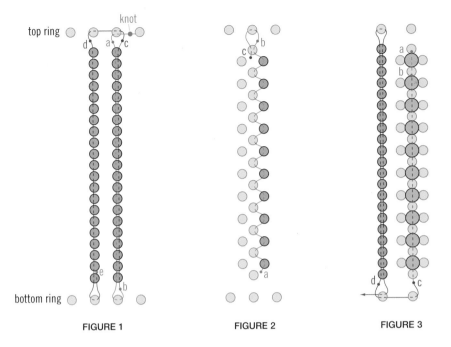

FIGURE 1

FIGURE 2

FIGURE 3

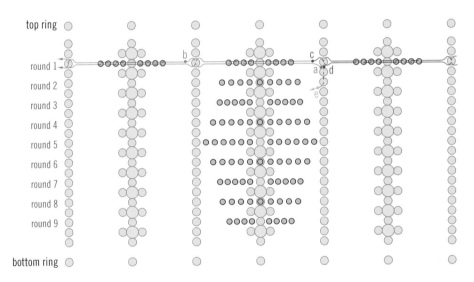

FIGURE 4

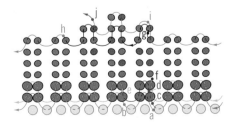

FIGURE 5

stitch in rounds 3–5, then decreasing by one A 14º per stitch in rounds 6–9. End the thread.

Tendril and stem

[1] Make a wrapped loop (Basics) 3 in. (7.6cm) from the end of a 15-in. (38cm) piece of wire. Do not cut the excess wrapping wire. Instead, coil it to within ¼ in. (6mm) of the wrapped stem to form a tendril. Set aside.

[2] Add a new thread (Basics) on the top ring, and exit any bead (figure 5, point a). Pick up two color B 11º seed beads, skip the next bead in the top ring, and sew through the next (a–b). Continue around the top ring, adding six more sets of beads (b–c). Sew through the first bead added in this round to get into position for round 2 (c–d). Insert the wire through the wooden bead, positioning the tendril between two sets of beads (photo b). Coil the other end of the wire so it is snug against the bead (photo c).

[3] Working in tubular herringbone stitch (Basics), pick up two B 11ºs, and sew down through the next bead in the previous round and up through the following bead (d–e). Repeat around, sewing over the tendril wire. Step up to begin round 3 (e–f).

[4] Work four rounds of herringbone using a mix of color B and color C 14º seed beads, stepping up at the end of each round.

[5] Work three stitches (g–h). Sew through the next four sets of beads without adding any beads, and step up (h–i).

[6] Sew through the first set of beads without adding any beads, then work one stitch (i–j). End the thread.

[7] Thread a ribbon or wire hook (see "Ornament hangers," p. 9) through the wrapped loop next to the stem to hang the pumpkin.

Dainty peyote stitch Russian ornament

by **Paula Adams**

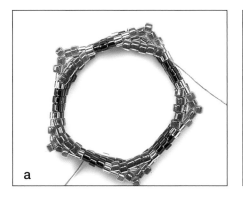

a

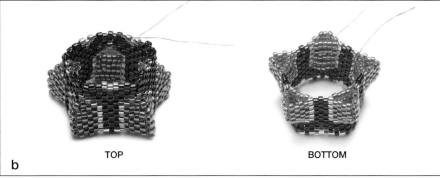

TOP

BOTTOM

b

round 5
round 6
round 7
round 8

FIGURE 1

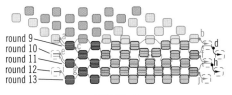

round 9
round 10
round 11
round 12
round 13

FIGURE 2

Stitch an exotic ornament by working rapid increases and decreases in tubular peyote stitch. Add a sparkling cascade of crystal fringe for a festive look. After the holiday season, hang your ornament from a fan pull or drapery tieback to enjoy it year-round.

step by step

Bottom half

[1] On 4 yd. (3.7m) of conditioned thread (Basics, p. 6) or Fireline, center a repeating pattern of seven color A and three color B cylinder beads five times for a total of 50 beads. Sew through them again to form a ring, and exit the third A.

[2] Using As, work two rounds of tubular, even-count peyote stitch (Basics), stepping up at the end of each round.

[3] Continue in peyote stitch, working the repeating pattern indicated below for each round and stepping up at the end of each round:

Round 5: Work four stitches with an A and one with a B (figure 1, a–b).

Round 6: Work three stitches with an A and two with a B (c–d).

Round 7: Work two stitches with an A and one with a B. Begin forming the points by working an increase with two Cs. Then work one stitch with a B (e–f).

Round 8: Work one A, one B, three Cs (splitting the increase), and one B (g–h).

[4] Work a support round inside the point: Sew through the beadwork to exit the B prior to the first point. Pick up five Cs and sew through the next B. Sew through the beads in the round to exit the B prior to the next point. Repeat around the ring. End with your thread exiting the B after the last point. Red beads were used in **photo a** to show the support round.

The round following a support round will always start with the thread exiting a B after a point.

Round 9: Work two A stitches and four C stitches (figure 2, a–b).

Round 10: Work an A, a B, a C, and then work an increase with two Cs. Work a C and a B (c–d). Repeat around the ring, step up, and then work a support round.

Round 11: Work two A stitches and five C stitches (e–f).

materials

- crystals:
  10 13mm faceted teardrops
  10 6mm or 4mm rounds or bicones
  10 6mm faceted rondelles
  10 5mm or 3mm bicones
  10–11 4mm bicones
- 4mm or 5mm round bead
- Japanese cylinder beads:
  4g in each of **2** colors: A, C
  3g in each of **2** colors: B, D
- 3 in. (7.6cm) 20- to 22-gauge wire
- nylon beading thread, conditioned with beeswax, or Fireline 6 lb. test
- beading needles, #12
- chainnose pliers
- roundnose pliers
- wire cutters

round 14
round 15
round 16
round 17
round 18
round 19
round 20
round 21

FIGURE 3

round 24
round 25
round 26
round 27
round 28
round 29

FIGURE 4

round 9
round 8
round 7
round 6
round 5
round 4
round 3
round 2
round 1

FIGURE 6

FIGURE 5

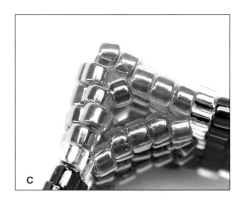

c

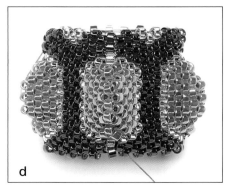

d

Round 12: Work an A, a B, four Cs, and a B (g–h). Repeat around the ring, step up, and work a support round.

Rounds 13–16: Repeat rounds 11 and 12 twice (photo b).

Round 17: Work two C stitches, decrease by sewing through the next two Cs, then work two C stitches and two A stitches (figure 3, a–b).

Round 18: Work three C stitches (stitching the second C in the decrease), a B, an A, and a B (c–d and photo c). Repeat around, step up, and work a support round.

Round 19: Work two A stitches, a B, two Cs, and a B (e–f).

Round 20: Work two A stitches and a B, work a decrease by sewing through two Cs, and then work a B and an A (g–h).

Round 21: Work two As, a B in the decrease, and two As (i–j).

Rounds 22 and 23: Work two rounds with As only (photo d).

Round 24: Work three As, a B, and an A (figure 4, a–b).

Round 25: Work two As, two Bs, and an A (c–d).

Round 26: Work an A and a B, decrease by sewing through two Bs, then work a B and an A (e–f).

Round 27: Work a B, a D (in the decrease), a B, and an A (g–h and photo e).

Round 28: Work two Ds and two Bs (i–j).

Round 29: Work a D, a C, a B, and a C (k–l).

Round 30: Work the round with Cs, totaling 20 beads (figure 5, a–b).

Round 31: Work a C, a B, a C, and a D (b–c).

Round 32: Work two Bs and two Ds (c–d).

Round 33: Decrease by sewing through the next two Bs (d–e), then work a B, a D, and a B (e–f).

Round 34: Work two Bs (g–h), then decrease by sewing through the next four Bs (h–i).

Round 35: Work a B, then sew the next six Bs (j–k).

[5] End the thread (Basics).

Top half

[1] Turn the beadwork over, thread a needle on the tail, and stitch the top half of the ornament in peyote stitch as follows, working the repeating pattern for each round as indicated (refer to figure 6 as you work rounds 1–9):

Round 1: Work a B, two As, and a B, decreasing by sewing through two Bs. After adding the last B, step up through three Bs.

Round 2: Work a B, an A, a B, and a D (in the decrease, as shown in photo e).

Round 3: Work two Bs and two Ds.

Round 4: Work a B, a C, a D, and a C.

Round 5: Work a round of Cs only.

Round 6: Work three Cs and a B.

Round 7: Work two Cs and two Bs.

Round 8: Work a C and a B, decrease by sewing through two Bs, and work a B.

Round 9: Work a B, a D in the decrease, and a B.

Round 10: Work two Ds and a B.

Round 11: Work a D and two As.

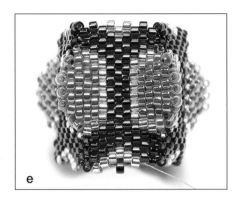

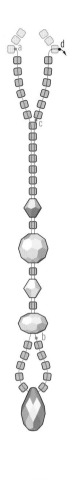

FIGURE 7

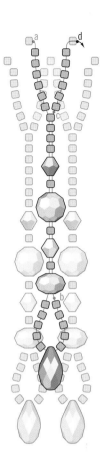

FIGURE 8

Round 12: Work an A, a B, and an A.

Round 13: Work two Bs and an A.

Round 14: Sew through two Bs to decrease, then work two Bs.

Round 15: Work a B and a D in the decrease.

Round 16: Work a round with Cs only.

Round 17: Work a C and a B.

Round 18: Work a round with Bs only.

Round 19: Sew through two Bs to decrease, then work a B.

Rounds 20 and 21: Work a round with As only.

[2] Sew through the five As on the last round again, and snug them in a tight ring. End the thread.

Finishing

[1] Make a wrapped loop (Basics) at one end of a 3-in. (7.6cm) piece of wire. String a 4mm or 5mm round bead and the ornament, bottom end first. Position the wrapped loop and bead below the last round on the bottom of the

ornament. String a 4mm bicone crystal if desired, and make a wrapped loop **(photo f)**. Thread a ribbon or wire hook (see "Ornament hangers," p. 9) through the loop to hang the ornament.

[2] To add fringe: Add 1 yd. (.9m) of thread in the beadwork near the bottom edge of the ornament, and exit a B at one of the points **(figure 7, point a)**. Pick up 13 Bs, a 4mm bicone, a B, a 5mm or 3mm bicone, a B, a 6mm or 4mm crystal, a B, a 6mm rondelle, five Bs, a teardrop-shaped crystal, and five Bs **(a–b)**. Skip the ten Bs and the teardrop, and sew back through the fringe beads, exiting the seventh B above the 4mm **(b–c)**. Pick up six Bs and sew through the B at the next point **(c–d)**. Repeat with the remaining points.

[3] Sew through to the edge B between two points **(figure 8, point a)**. Pick up ten Bs and the fringe pattern from the 4mm bicone to the Bs after the teardrop **(a–b)**. Skip the ten Bs and the teardrop,

and sew back through the fringe beads, exiting the fourth B above the 4mm bicone **(b–c)**. Pick up six Bs and sew through the corresponding B on the other side of the point **(c–d)**. Repeat with the remaining points.

[4] End the thread.

EDITOR'S NOTE:
Keep your tension tight as you work the decrease sections and the support rows. The beads fit snugly, so your matte beads may tend to break.

Flip-flop style

by **Diane Hertzler**

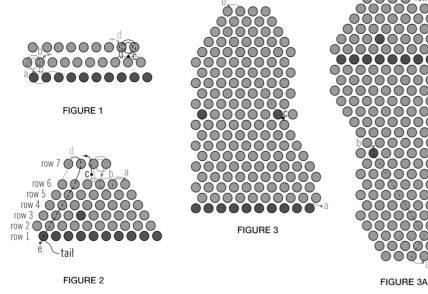

FIGURE 1

FIGURE 2

FIGURE 3

FIGURE 3A

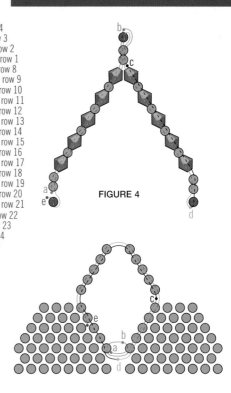

FIGURE 4

FIGURE 5

When autumn ushers in the chilly days of fall, I am always surprised to see people still wearing flip-flops. I guess they don't want to see summer end! Worked in brick stitch and embellished with crystals, this darling decoration will bring the warmth of summer indoors all year.

stepbystep

Soles

Figure 3A is a graph of the sole. The dark beads (shown to clarify the directions) on figures 1, 2, 3, and 4 correspond to the dark beads on figure 3A.

[1] Working with 11º seed beads on a comfortable length of thread, make a bead ladder (Basics, p. 6) 10 beads long.

[2] Continue in brick stitch as follows:
Row 2: Begin the row with an increase (figure 1, a–b), and then work eight regular stitches.
Row 3: Begin with a decrease (c–d), then work seven regular stitches.
Rows 4–6: Repeat row 3, decreasing each row by one bead (figure 2).
Row 7: Sew down through the second and up through the third bead in the previous row (a–b). Pick up two 11ºs, sew through them again, and sew under the thread bridge between the third and fourth beads in the previous row (b–c). Work two more stitches. Sew through the beadwork to exit the end bead in the ladder (d–e and figure 3, point a). Thread a needle on the tail, sew into the beadwork, and trim.
Rows 8–26: Flip your work so row 1 is on top. Continue in brick stitch to

the end of the heel, increasing and decreasing as needed. Sew through the sole to **point c (figure 3, b–c).**

[3] Repeat steps 1 and 2 for a second sole.

Thong

[1] With the working thread on one sole, pick up a 11º, then a repeating pattern of one 11º and one 3mm crystal five times. Pick up two 11ºs, and sew through the bead on the sole where the thong should connect to the toe area **(figure 4, a–b).**

[2] Sew back through the two 11ºs **(b–c).**

[3] Pull snug. Pick up a repeating pattern of one 3mm and one 11º five times, then pick up one 11º and sew through the other connection point on the sole **(c–d).**

[4] Retrace the thread path in the thong **(d–e).** End the thread in the sole (Basics).

[5] Turn the second sole over so it is a mirror image of the first, and repeat steps 1–4 to make the thong.

Assembly

[1] Place the flip-flops side by side. Add a new thread (Basics), and sew to exit at **figure 5, point a.**

[2] Sew through the corresponding bead in the second sole **(a–b).**

[3] Sew through the bead in the first sole again, the corresponding bead in

the second sole, and the next four beads in the heel **(b–c).**

[4] Pick up 10 11ºs, and sew through five beads in the other heel **(c–d).**

[5] Retrace the thread path through the loop **(d–e).** End the thread.

Finishing

[1] Place the flip-flops on a piece of waxed paper. Flatten the soles with your fingers if needed.

[2] Paint the soles with a coat of floor polish, allowing the liquid to saturate the thread. Let dry to a hard finish.

[3] Thread a ribbon or wire hook (see "Ornament hangers," p. 9) through the loop between the flip-flops' soles to hang the ornament.

materials

- 20 3mm bicone crystals, purple
- 6g size 11º seed beads, green
- nylon beading thread, size B, green
- beading needles, #10
- artist's acrylic paintbrush, approx. size 4
- Future floor polish
- 3-in. (7.6cm) square of waxed paper

Chevron heart

by **Diane Hertzler**

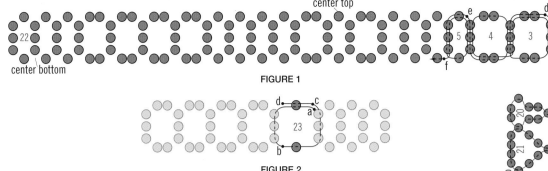

FIGURE 1

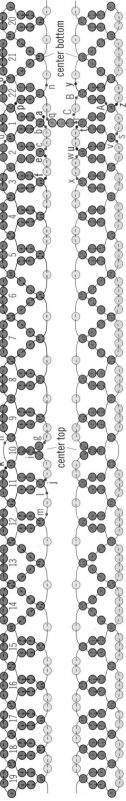

FIGURE 2

Valentine's Day is a wonderful time of year to say, "I love you" to the special people in our lives. Giving this three-sided heart ornament, which combines multiple stitches and fringing techniques, is a clever way to make that statement.

step by step

Inner wall

The inner wall of the heart will be stitched in right-angle weave (Basics, p. 6). Each vertical column has three beads. Between each vertical column, there are one or two beads.

Unit 1: On a comfortable length of thread, pick up 10 color A 11° seed beads, leaving a 6-in. (15cm) tail. Sew through the beads again to form a ring, and tie the working thread and tail with a square knot (Basics). Sew through the next five As (**figure 1, a–b**).

Unit 2: Pick up seven As, and, working in right-angle weave, sew through the three beads in the previous unit your thread exited at the start of this step (**b–c**). Sew through the next five As (**c–d**).

Units 3 and **4:** Repeat unit 2 (**d–e**).

Unit 5: Work as in unit 2, but pick up only five As (**e–f**).

Units 6–22: Follow **figure 1** to determine whether to pick up five or seven As for the remaining stitches of the inner wall.

Unit 23: Connect unit 1 to unit 22: Pick up an A, and sew through three As in unit 1 (**figure 2, a–b**). Pick up an A, and sew through three As in unit 22 (**b–c**). Sew through the first A added in this step (**c–d**).

Front surface

The front will be stitched using chevron chain. It is sewn to the horizontal beads of the inside wall as you work around the graph. The ornament will be woven with red beads; however, the figure shows the inside wall beads as blue and the chevron chain beads as red.

Loop 1: Pick up nine As, and sew back through the first bead picked up (**figure 3, a–b**). Sew through the next two horizontal As in the inner wall (**b–c**).

Loop 2: Pick up three As, and sew through the seventh A of the previous loop (**c–d**). Pick up five As, and sew back through the first A picked up in this loop (**d–e**). Sew through the next two horizontal beads in the inner wall (**e–f**).

Loops 3–9: Repeat loop 2, noting the bead count changes in the horizontal beads of the inner wall and the horizontal beads at the top of each loop (**f–g**).

Loop 10: This is the center top of the heart. Pick up three As and sew through the bead shown (**g–h**). Pick up one A, and sew back through two As (**h–i**). Pick up one A and sew through two horizontal As in the inner wall (**i–j**).

Loop 11: Pick up three As, and sew through the bead shown (**j–k**). Pick up six As, and sew back through the first bead picked up in this loop (**k–l**). Sew through one horizontal bead in the inner wall (**l–m**).

materials

- **23** 5mm bugle beads, gold
- **23** 4mm bicone crystals, red
- **23** 3mm bicone crystals, red
- **10g** size 11° seed beads, color A, red
- **4g** size 11° seed beads, color B, gold
- nylon beading thread, size B
- beading needles, #10

FIGURE 3

FIGURE 4

edge beads

center bottom

FIGURE 5

Loops 12–21: Repeat loop 2, noting the bead count changes as indicated in **m–n**.
Loop 22: Pick up three As, and sew through the bead shown from the previous loop **(n–o)**. Pick up two As, and sew through the forth bead strung in loop 1 **(o–p)**. Pick up two As, and sew through the first bead picked up in this loop and one horizontal bead **(p–q)**. Sew through the next three As in the inside wall to the other side of the ornament **(q–r)**.

Back surface

The beads that will be added to this side are shown as brown beads in **figure 3**, and they will be used to connect the remaining edge of the inner wall and the front surface.
[1] Pick up four As, and sew through the two As at the top of loop 1 **(r–s)**. Pick up three As, and sew back through the first A picked up in this step **(s–t)**. Sew through the next two horizontal As **(t–u)**.
[2] Pick up three As, and sew through the bead shown **(u–v)**. Sew through two As, pick up three As, and sew back through the first A picked up in this step **(v–w)**. Sew through the next two horizontal beads **(w–x)**.
[3] Continue around, connecting the inner wall to the top edge of the heart **(x–y)**.
[4] Pick up three As and sew through the next two As **(y–z)**. Sew through the A picked up in step 1 **(z–A)**. Pick up two As and sew through the first A picked up in this step **(A–B)**. Sew through the next horizontal bead **(B–C)**.

Accent beads

[1] Pick up one color B 11º seed bead, and sew through the next two

horizontal As **(figure 4, a–b)**. Pick up one B, and sew through the next two horizontal beads **(b–c)**. Continue around, adding one B at the end of each set of vertical beads and exit the bead shown at **point d**.
[2] Sew through the three vertical beads and the next two horizontal beads **(d–e)**. Repeat step 1 to add Bs around the other side of the inner wall.
[3] Sew through to the outside edge **(f–g)**. Add one B between each set of horizontal beads. When you reach the center bottom, sew through two As, pick up one B, and sew through the next two As. End the thread (Basics).

Fringe and finishing

The fringe will be added to each of the 23 edge beads marked with a •
on **figure 5**. Add a new thread (Basics), and sew through the outer edge to exit **(figure 5, point a)**.
[1] Pick up one B, three As, one B, three As, one B, three As, one bugle bead, one A, one B, one 3mm crystal, one B, one A, one B, one 4mm crystal, and five Bs **(a–b)**. Skip the five Bs, and sew back through the rest of the fringe **(b–c)**. Sew through two edge beads **(c–d)**.
[2] Repeat step 1, adding 22 more fringes to the beads along the edge of the ornament. End the thread.
[3] Attach a ribbon or wire hook (see "Ornament hangers," p. 9) to hang the heart.

Ice crystals

by **Diane Jolie**

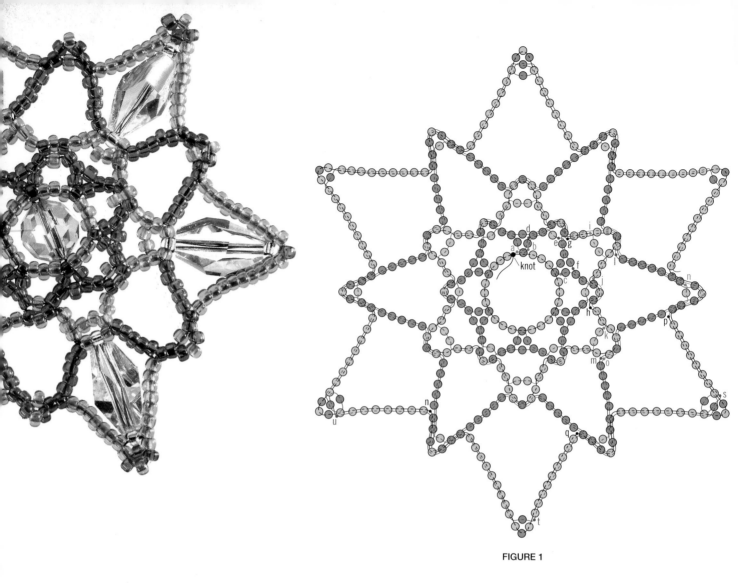

FIGURE 1

If you enjoy creating handmade ornaments, you'll love these snowflakes. They work up quickly in 11º seed beads, so there's time to make several, even during the busiest holiday season. There's no need to put them in storage when the holidays are over. These ornaments will look wonderful hanging in a sunny window all winter long.

stepbystep

[1] Thread a needle with 7 ft. (2.1m) of Fireline or conditioned nylon beading thread (Basics, p. 6).

Round 1: Pick up a repeating pattern of one color A 11º seed bead and three color B 11ºs six times, leaving a 6-in. (15cm) tail. Tie the beads in a ring with a square knot (Basics), and sew through the first A again (figure 1, a–b).

Round 2: Pick up four As, a B, and four As. Sew through the second A in the ring (b–c). Repeat around the ring until you have a total of six loops. Step up through the first A in this round (c–d).

Round 3: Sew through the next two As in round 2, and pick up a B (d–e). Sew through two As in round 2, and pick up an A (e–f). Repeat around, then step up through three As, a B, and an A on round 2 (f–g).

Round 4: Pick up four Bs, a color C 11º, and four Bs. Sew through an A, a B, and an A in round 2 (g–h). Repeat around, then step up through the first two Bs added in round 4 (h–i).

Round 5: Pick up two Bs. Skip the next five beads in round 4, and sew through the following two Bs (i–j). Sew through an A, a B, and an A in round 2 and through two Bs on round 4 (j–k). Repeat around, then step up through two Bs, a C, and a B in round 4 (k–l).

Round 6: Pick up eight As, a B, and eight As. Sew through a B, a C, and a B in round 4 (l–m). Repeat around, then step up through the first seven As in the new round (m–n).

Round 7: Pick up one B and sew through seven As, a B, a C, and a B (n–o). Repeat around, and step up through eight As, a B, and three As (o–p).

Round 8: Pick up eight Bs, an A, a B, an A, and eight Bs, and sew through three As, a B, and three As (p–q). Pick up ten Bs, an A, and ten Bs, and sew through three As, a B, and three As (q–r). Repeat around, and step up through the first eight Bs in the round (r–s).

Round 9: Pick up an A, and sew through a B. Pick up a C, and sew through the B,

82

materials

- **6** 12 x 8mm crystals
- 8mm round crystal
- size 11º Japanese seed beads:
  2g color A
  2g color B
  1g color C
- nylon beading thread, conditioned with beeswax, or Fireline 8 lb. test
- beading needles, #12
- Future floor polish or varnish
- small paintbrush

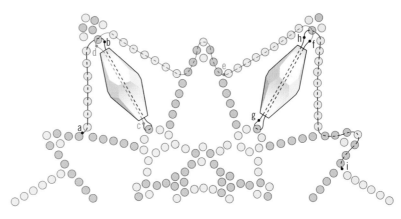

FIGURE 2

the A, and the B again. Then sew through seven Bs, three As, a B, three As, and nine Bs (s–t). Pick up a C, and sew through nine Bs, three As, a B, three As, and eight Bs (t–u). Repeat around.

[2] Sew through seven Bs in round 8 and a C in round 9 (figure 2, a–b). Pick up a 12 x 8mm crystal, and sew through a C in round 4 (b–c). Sew back through the crystal (c–d), then sew through the C in round 9, seven Bs on round 8, and three As, a B, and three As in round 6 (d–e).

[3] Sew through nine Bs in round 8 and a C in round 9 (e–f). Pick up a 12 x 8mm crystal, and sew through a C in round 4 (f–g). Sew back through the crystal (g–h), then sew through the C in round 9, nine Bs in round 8, and three As, a B, and three As on round 6 (h–i).

[4] Repeat steps 2 and 3 twice, and end the thread (Basics).

[5] With the 6-in. (15cm) tail, pick up an 8mm crystal, and sew through the opposite A in the first round (figure 3, a–b). Sew back through the 8mm crystal and the first A (b–c). Retrace the thread path, and end the tail.

[6] With a paintbrush, coat the seed beads, not the crystals, with varnish or floor polish to stiffen them. Let dry, then coat the other side.

[7] Attach a ribbon, monofilament, or wire hook (see "Ornament hangers," p. 9) to hang the snowflake.

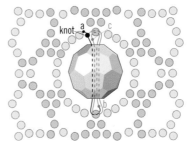

FIGURE 3

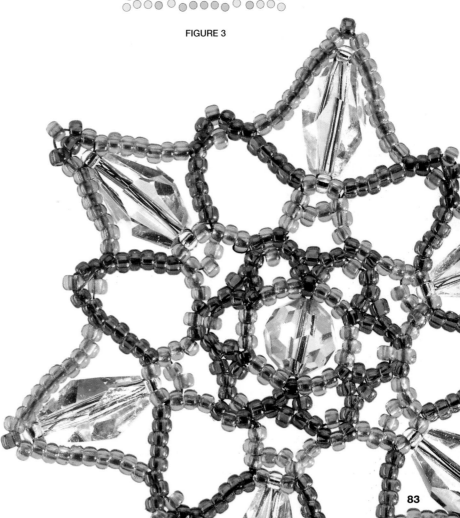

Sweet treat

by **Diane Hertzler**

While shopping in a local candy emporium, a dish of ribbon candy caught my eye, and my mind immediately began processing the shape and colors with beads. This project offers a festive ornament created by weaving flat, odd-count peyote stitch with two needles.

step by step

[1] Thread a #10 needle at one end of a comfortable length of thread, and thread a #12 needle at the opposite end.
[2] Continue as follows:
Rows 1 and 2: Following the pattern in **figure 1**, pick up 19 11º cylinder beads, and center them on the thread.
Row 3: With the #12 needle, work in flat, odd-count peyote stitch (see "Working flat, odd-count peyote," p. 86) across the row **(figure 1, a–b)**. Pick up the last bead in the row, and pull it into place **(b–c)**. Drop the #12 needle, and pick up the #10 needle.
Row 4: Sew through the bead just added **(d–e)**. Work across the row in peyote stitch **(e–f)**.
Row 5: Work peyote stitch back across the row **(f–g)**. Pick up the last bead in the row, and pull it into place **(g–h)**. Drop the #10 needle, and pick up the #12 needle.
Row 6: Work as in row 4 with the #12 needle.
Row 7: Work as in row 5 with the #12 needle.

materials

- size 11º cylinder beads:
  10g pink
  6g white
  6g orange
  2g green
- 4 in. (10cm) 20-gauge craft wire
- nylon beading thread, size B, pink
- beading needles, #10 and #12
- artist's acrylic paintbrush, approx. size 4
- 2 drinking straws
- Future floor polish
- magnetic board (optional)
- 3 x 6-in. (7.6 x 15cm) piece of waxed paper
- roundnose pliers
- wire cutters

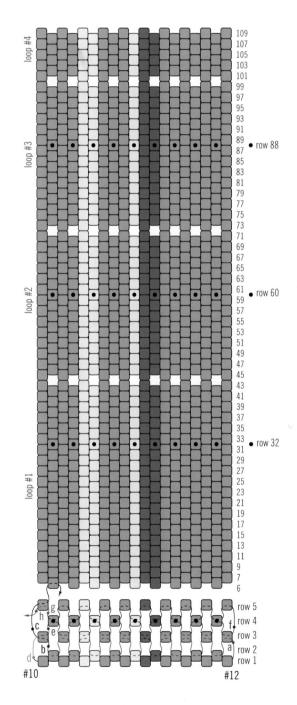

FIGURE 1

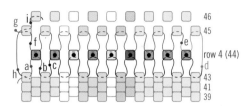

FIGURE 2

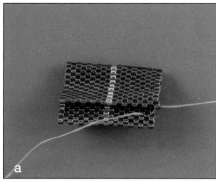

a

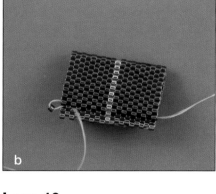

b

WORKING FLAT, ODD-COUNT PEYOTE

Odd-count peyote is the same as even-count peyote (Basics, p. 6), except for the turn on odd-numbered rows, where the last bead of the row can't be attached in the usual way because there is no up-bead to sew through.

Begin as for flat even-count peyote, but pick up an odd number of beads. Work row 3 as in even-count, stopping before adding the last two beads.

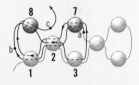

Work a figure 8 turn at the end of row 3: Pick up the next-to-last bead (#7), and sew through #2, then #1 (a–b). Pick up the last bead of the row (#8), and sew through #2, #3, #7, #2, #1, and #8 (b–c).

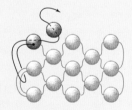

You can work this turn at the end of each odd-numbered row, but this edge will be stiffer than the other. Instead, in subsequent odd-numbered rows, pick up the last bead of the row, then sew under the thread bridge immediately below. Sew back through the last bead added to begin the next row.

Row 8: Work as in row 4 with the #10 needle.
Row 9: Work as in row 5 with the #10 needle.
Rows 10–43: Continue working as in rows 6–9.

Connecting

Row 44: No beads will be added. Row 43 will be "zipped" to row 4. Fold the strip over and lay row 43 on top of row 5. Sew through the first bead in row 4 (photo a and figure 2, a–b). Sew through the second bead in row 43 (b–c). Continue zipping across the row (c–d).
Row 45: Pick up the first bead in the row, and sew through the last bead in row 4 (photo b and d–e). Continue in peyote stitch across the row (e–f). Pick up the last bead in the row, and pull it into place (f–g). Switch needles, sew through the bead just added, and pick up a new bead (h–i).
Rows 46–71: Continue working as in rows 10–43 to create beadwork that will form the second loop.
Rows 72 and 73: Repeat rows 44 and 45 to connect rows 72 and 73 to row 32.
Rows 74–268: Work until you have nine loops, connecting them as follows:
    Loop 3: Connect row 100 to row 60.
    Loop 4: Connect row 128 to row 88.
    Loop 5: Connect row 156 to row 116.
    Loop 6: Connect row 184 to row 144.
    Loop 7: Connect row 212 to row 172.
    Loop 8: Connect row 240 to row 200.
    Loop 9: Connect row 268 to row 228.

Loop 10

Rows 269–289: For the final loop, work as before for 20 rows.
Row 290: Work four stitches (figure 3, a–b). Sew through two beads (b–c), and finish the row (c–d).
Row 291: Work four stitches (d–e). Pick up three beads, and sew through the next up bead (e–f). Finish the row (f–g), and switch needles.
Row 292: Work four stitches (h–i). Sew through the three beads added over the gap (i–j). Finish the row (j–k).
Row 293: Work peyote stitch to add five beads (k–l). Sew through the middle bead of the three beads added (l–m). Finish the row (m–n). Switch needles.
Rows 294 and 295: Work peyote stitch as before.
Rows 296 and 297: Work as before to connect row 296 to 256.

Point

Rows 298 and 299: Work peyote stitch as before.
Row 300: Work across the row, adding only nine beads (figure 4, a–b). To turn, sew under the thread bridge between rows 297 and 299. Sew back through the bead exited and last bead added (b–c).
Row 301: Work across the row, adding only eight beads (c–d). To turn, sew under the thread between the bead exited and the bead diagonally below. Sew back through the bead exited and the last bead added (d–e).
Rows 302–308: Repeat row 301 seven times, decreasing the number of beads in each row so that row 308 is a single bead. End the threads.

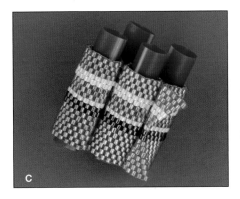

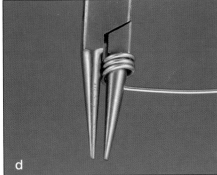

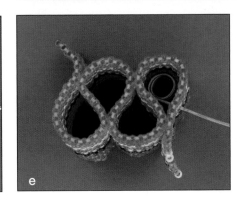

V end

[1] Add a new thread (Basics) at the beginning of the ornament. Sew through the beadwork to exit at **figure 5, point a.**

Rows A and B: Work peyote stitch to add eight new beads in two rows as shown **(a–b).** To turn, sew under the thread bridge between rows 1 and A, then sew back through the bead just exited and the last bead added **(b–c).**

Rows C–H: Repeat rows A and B, decreasing the number of beads in each row, so that row H is a single bead. Add a new thread as before, and sew through the beadwork to exit at **point d.**

Rows I and J: Work in peyote to add eight new beads in two rows as shown **(d–e).**

To turn, sew under the thread bridge between rows 1 and I, then sew back through the bead just exited and the last

bead added **(e–f).**

Rows K–P: Repeat rows I and J, decreasing the number of beads in each row so that row P is a single bead.

[2] End the threads.

Finishing

[1] Cut the straws into ten 1¼-in. (3.2cm) sections, and place one section into each loop of the ornament **(photo c).**

[2] Paint the ornament with floor polish, allowing the threads to absorb the liquid. Place the ornament straw-ends down on waxed paper, and let dry.

[3] Remove the straw sections when the ornament has dried to a hard finish.

Hanging loop

[1] Cut a 4-in. (10cm) piece of 20-gauge wire. Wrap one end of the wire three

times around the widest part of the jaws of a pair of roundnose pliers **(photo d).**

[2] Insert the straight end of the wire into the last loop of the ornament and through the hole created in loop 10 to exit the top of the ornament **(photo e).**

[3] Create a hanging loop on the top of the ornament by making another three-coil wrap as before. Thread a ribbon or wire hook (see "Ornament hangers," p. 9) through the loop to hang the candy.

DESIGNER'S TIP:

Try placing your graphs on a magnetic board with a straight edge or ruler. This will enable you to maintain your place in the pattern.

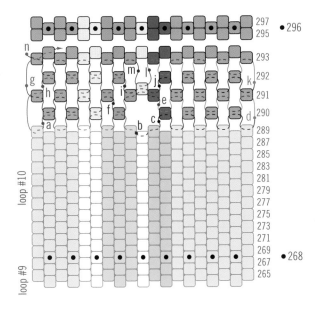

FIGURE 3

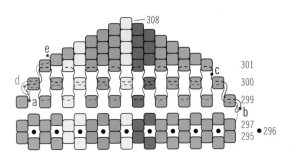

FIGURE 4

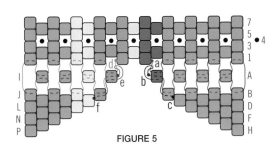

FIGURE 5

Creative twist

by **Diane Hertzler**

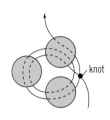

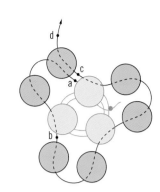

FIGURE 1

FIGURE 2

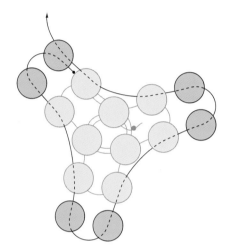

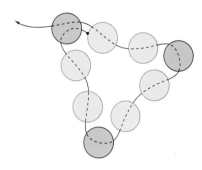

FIGURE 3

FIGURE 4

After taking a class at the *Bead&Button* Show with Rachel Cotugno on making decorative shapes from herringbone tubes, I designed this easy pretzel. Add salt to your pretzel with clear, silver-lined beads, and hang it on your Christmas tree or use it to deck out your kitchen any time.

step by step

If you are using two colors of 11º seed beads, mix them together so you pick up the colors randomly as you stitch.

[1] On a comfortable length of conditioned thread (Basics, p. 6), pick up three 11ºs, and sew through the beads again, leaving a 6-in. (15cm) tail.
[2] Pull the beads into a ring, tie the tail and working thread together with a square knot (Basics), and sew through the next bead in the ring **(figure 1)**.
[3] Pick up two 11ºs, and sew through the next bead in the ring **(figure 2, a–b)**. Repeat twice **(b–c)**, then sew

through the first bead added in this round **(c–d)**.
[4] Work in tubular herringbone (Basics and **figure 3**) until the tube is about 8 in. (20cm) long. Keep the tension tight as you work. Pull the beads together so they stack above the previous round. The beads will start to form a tube after the fourth round.
[5] Slide an 8-in. (20cm) piece of wire into the tube.
[6] Work one more round, adding one bead per stitch **(figure 4)**. Sew through the three beads just added, and cinch them together to close the end of the tube. Tie several half-hitch knots (Basics) between beads, but don't trim the thread.

materials
- Japanese seed beads:
  8g size 11º, in **1** or **2** topaz colors (pretzel)
  4g size 10º, clear silver-lined (salt)
- 8 in. (20cm) 18- or 16-gauge wire
- nylon beading thread, conditioned with beeswax
- beading needles, #10 or #12

[7] Form the tube into a pretzel shape.
[8] To add the salt, position the thread so it exits a bead on the front of the beadwork. Embellish the surface with size 10º seed beads, stitching beads randomly and in different directions. Weave through the herringbone tube as you add the salt beads to make sure your thread doesn't show between beads.
[9] Attach a colorful ribbon or a wire hook (see "Ornament hangers," p. 9) to hang your pretzel.

Fan wheel flakes

by **Maria Rypan**

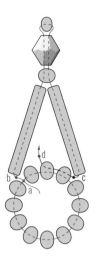

FIGURE 1

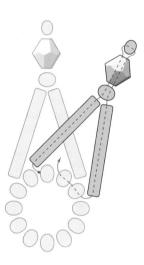

FIGURE 2

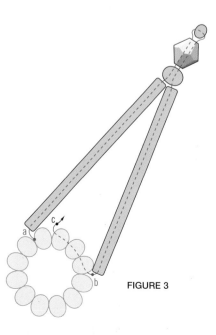

FIGURE 3

My modification of a unique beadwork style from Ukraine resulted in this beautiful circular fan ornament with 12 overlapping points. These are so much fun to make, you'll hope for cold weather so you can stay inside and bead.

step by step

Small snowflake

[1] Thread a needle on one end of 4½ ft. (1.4m) of flexible beading wire. String 12 8º seed beads, leaving a 5-in. (13cm) tail. Tie the beads into a ring with a square knot (Basics, p. 6, and **figure 1, a–b**).

[2] Pick up a 15mm bugle bead, an 8º, a 6mm crystal, and an 11º seed bead. Skip the 11º, sew back through the 6mm and the 8º, and pick up a bugle **(b–c)**.

[3] Skip the next three 8ºs in the ring, and sew back through the third and second beads skipped **(c–d)**.

[4] Repeat steps 2 and 3 **(figure 2)** around the ring until there are 12 points. As you work each point, make sure you place the new point on top of the previous one. This will be the front surface. When you finish the 11th and 12th points, sew into the ring from the back surface, and exit the front surface.

[5] Sew through a few beads in the ring, end the beading wire (Basics), and trim. Repeat with the tail.

[6] String clear monofilament or metallic thread through an 11º at the end of one of the points to make a hanging loop.

Large snowflake

[1] Using 5 ft. (1.5m) of beading wire, follow step 1 of "Small snowflake," substituting 6º seed beads for the 8ºs.

[2] Follow step 2 of "Small snowflake," substituting 6ºs for the 8ºs and 30mm bugle beads for the 15mms **(figure 3, a–b)**.

[3] Skip the next four 6ºs in the ring, and sew back through the fourth, third, and second beads skipped **(b–c)**.

[4] Follow steps 4–6 of "Small snowflake."

materials

both snowflakes
- flexible beading wire, .010
- beading needles, #10
- wire cutters or scissors
- clear monofilament or metallic thread

small snowflake (2⅛ in./5.4cm)
- 24 15mm bugle beads
- 12 6mm bicone crystals
- 24 size 8º seed beads
- 12 size 10º or 11º seed beads

large snowflake (3½ in./8.9cm)
- 24 30mm bugle beads
- 12 6mm bicone crystals
- 24 size 6º seed beads
- 12 size 10º or 11º seed beads

EDITOR'S NOTE:
As you work, the points of the snowflake may fold up like a fan. Hold the snowflake by the center to minimize this movement.

DESIGN GUIDELINES:
- To change the size of the snowflake, use any size bugle beads, then choose seed beads and crystals to suit. The snowflakes shown opposite were made with (clockwise from top right) vintage 60mm bugles, 15mm bugles, and 30mm bugles.
- Adjust the angle of the points by changing the number of seed beads you go through.
- You may need to flatten the tip of your flexible beading wire to get it to fit through your beading needle.
- You can also use snowflakes to spruce up holiday packages or napkin rings.

What a lifesaver!

by **Diane Hertzler**